# SWIPING RIGHT

NEW DEGREE PRESS



SWIPING RIGHT

*How We Connect, Communicate, and Love*

ISBN 978-1-64137-054-7 *Paperback*

ISBN 978-1-64137-055-4 *Ebook*

*To Daviree, for our conversation over coffee on December 2, 2016*

# CONTENTS


INTRODUCTION ........ 1

1. ATTACHMENT THEORY ........ 5
2. THE WAITLIST ........ 19
3. A SOCIAL PHENOMENON ........ 31
4. RAPID REWARDS ........ 41
5. SUBTWEET ........ 51
6. TRIPLE DIGITS ........ 63
7. #IRL (IN REAL LIFE) ........ 77
8. SEX(TING) ........ 89
9. MANSPACE ........ 99
10. FAIRY TALES ........ 111
11. COMPATIBILITY ........ 127
12. DIGITAL TATTOOS ........ 139

CONCLUSION: THE POWER OF HELLO ........ 151

ACKNOWLEDGMENTS ........ 159

REFERENCES ........ 161

*There are many kinds of joy, but they all lead to one: the joy to be loved.*

—MICHAEL ENDE, AUTHOR,
*THE NEVERENDING STORY*

# INTRODUCTION

Welcome to social media! You have just joined a global community of...

over 2 billion active social media users,
the 88% of millennials that have a social media profile,
the 81% of Americans that have a social media profile,
the 2 billion monthly active Facebook users,
the 700 million active Instagram users,
the 7 million monthly active Tinder users,
the 18 million active Bumble users,
and you're likely on The League's waitlist of 250,000.

The most successful social media platforms are the ones created with an understanding psychology and how people think and operate. Social media developers create spaces for people to create their own social experiences and enjoy them. Social media has shifted our social behavior.

There is constant chatter about "Who liked my photos," "How many RT's did you get," or "I have X+ connections of LinkedIn." These questions are components of every-day conversations and is completely normalized in every-day life. Just think about how many news articles or stories you read that now feature a thread of "tweets" as a source for information and quotes. Additionally, online dating is now even included popular culture. If Carrie Bradshaw had Tinder, what would the Sex and the City storyline look like today?

In this digital world, you can connect with a man/woman from Boston while staying in D.C. and (s)he may be your "special someone." Social media has not only impacted dating, but also the human social experience.

The general consensus is that online dating applications and digital social platforms have skewed the ways in which millennials communicate and create healthy relationships. However, social media is a tool. Tinder is a tool that offers a pool of 100 prospective daters within a 50-mile radius, compared to the 10 considerably attractive people you see during a night out. Social media isn't the problem in this area of social interaction. People are the problem. Our innate human behaviors are the problem, and it's time to stop blaming social media for the lack of *love*, lack of commitment, and overt sensitivity of the new alleged "sex-craved" generation. But, rather analyze how social media has impacted millennials' behaviors.

In this book, you will learn how the best platforms are adapted to enhance our innate behaviors, not change them. People will always want to engage with others, and social media allows us to do so more efficiently and with more variety.

People now have more access to connections from around their cities, countries and the globe. The amount of opportunities that people are now able to engage in because of social media has expanded our social experiences and exposure to more identities, ideas, mindsets and viewpoints.

I've swiped, liked, retweeted, followed, shared, and all of the above again and again. I grew up hiding my MySpace page from my parents, getting in trouble on Facebook for posting things I thought I understood at 12, utilized every filter I could on Instagram, and as a college student, played all night on Tinder over a bottle of wine.

I am a millennial that understands what it's like to get a view on Snapchat and not get a text back. This is an effect of the social phenomenon. However, I'm here to tell you that social media are tools (not the end all be all) to creating lasting relationships in today's digital world. You'll learn the importance of how understanding healthy relationships offline will help you create better relationships online. From relationship consultants to psychology experts, to the stories of millennials themselves, this book will analyze what creating lasting relationships looks like in 2018.

Application creators are constantly evolving and changing the way their applications can create long-term relationships, whether it be social, romantic, or professional. However, it's not about them. It's about you. It's about your vulnerability, your authenticity, and your capability of being compatible with other people and the world around you. Subconsciously, in every daily interaction, you are metaphorically swiping right or left on that potential lover, potential friend, potential business partner, potential long-lasting decision, and many more.

Connecting with others is what makes us human. This book will explain how we connect with one another and the tools we now have at our disposal to do so. A new friend, lover, and connection is at our fingertips.

So, let's swipe right into it.

## CHAPTER 1

# ATTACHMENT THEORY

*A person's attachment status is a fundamental determinant of their relationships, and this is reflected in the way they feel about themselves and others . . . Where there is a secure core state, a person feels good about themselves and their capacity to be effective and pursue their projects. Where the core state is insecure, defensive strategies come into play.*

—JEREMY HOLMES, AUTHOR,
*JOHN BOWLBY AND THE ATTACHMENT THEORY*

Imagine trying to teach yourself mathematics. Each relationship is a lesson with a number of quizzes and a final exam at the end of the course. Based on your former self-taught lessons and maybe some help from your older sibling, who's only as versed in the subject as you are, you take a final exam on the topic. How well would you do? Learning how to navigate dating and relationships works the same way as learning a topic, like mathematics, except you have to teach yourself. The dates act as the quizzes. Based on your performance on these quizzes, you then must decipher what you did right and what you did wrong. When you finally find a single person that you want focus on, you then continuously study that subject until that final test. This test decides if this subject is going to become long-term study, or relationship. Without the adequate tools to prepare for your exam, you likely will not perform very well and have to start over again. You may even begin to notice a pattern in your performance in this topic. You question "what am I doing wrong?" and "why do I keep getting this wrong?" Well, just like math, you shouldn't have to teach yourself how to successfully navigate and grow healthy relationships.

Before I dive into how the online tools impacted my relationships as a millennial, it was important for me to understand how I engage offline. The attachment theory, developed by John Bowlby, teaches us how the relationships of our early childhood have impacted our relationships today.

It's a privilege to grow up seeing healthy relationships, and while no relationship is perfect, it's important to analyze how what we saw and felt growing up directly affects our relationships later in our lives.

* *

When I was six years old, my dad cheated on my mom. If you were to ask me about my family dynamic or even witness it in person, you would've never guessed this occurred. However, it's not a secret.

"How many siblings do you have, Devin?"

I generally answer with "I have 3 older brothers." This is the truth, but not the entire truth. I have a younger brother who is the result of my father's infidelity.

I still remember when our parents sat my three brothers and I down and told us what happened. All six of us were sitting on the bed, as we usually did when we had our frequent family meetings. I, of course, am laying between my parents, and specifically cuddled under my father, and begging my mom to rub my back. My three brothers were sprawled at different corners, all trying to fit on the king-sized mattress.

"We have to tell you guys something," said my father in a somber tone.

"Daddy broke the law," my mother exclaimed.

*Huh?*

"Is Daddy going to jail?" one of my brother's asked.

"Daddy will be in Mommy's jail," my mom replied.

*I still don't get it.*

"So when two people are married, they follow God's law. One of the laws is that Daddy will only love Mommy and Mommy will only love Daddy. Daddy broke that law."

*My six-year old mind kind of understood what was happening but was still slightly confused by the situation.*

"You all have another sibling."

*Whoa! I hope it's a girl. I have enough brothers.*

"You all have a little brother and he will be coming to visit us from time to time." I was shocked, and still slightly confused. I remember thinking, *how can I have a brother that needs to visit?* All my brothers lived with me. However, this one didn't. This brother was different; he wasn't my mom's child.

Seeing my younger brother for the first time made this situation all the more real. Even as a young child, I knew he was different from the rest of us. His presence was temporary and the house operated differently when he first came to visit. I noticed how my mom's mood was different that first time. In that moment, I fully realized and understood exactly what my father did and how this occurrence would affect my parents' marriage.

It's not like an elephant in our household or anything. It was just something that happened. And, my mom, who was the most affected as one can probably assume, decided to stay with my dad and work on their relationship. With the help of counseling and both of my parents' commitment to improving their relationship, my mom was able to move on in a positive direction and not resent my dad nor my little brother. She was even able to sit down with the other woman and make peace. My parents' relationship was never the same after that, but I only know that now that I've gotten older and my mom and I are able to have "girl chats." Still, my parents are deeply in love.

I was never hurt, saddened or confused by the situation as one might assume. I was so young when it occurred, and my parents handled the situation maturely and with a promise to each other that they would do whatever it took to not allow the drama to overshadow the love that filled our home. My parents conducted the family meeting during our summer break almost a year after my younger brother was born. They said they did this because they didn't want us to have any anxiety over the unknown of what was going to happen next.

They wanted to give us answers and have a plan in place. I see now as I navigate my own personal relationships how this occurrence has affected how I view relationships.

My mom chose to stay and work on her relationship. I'm sure she would have received a lot of support from friends and family if she had decided to end the marriage. My father gave her every opportunity to leave, promising to keep everything in place financially, being that she was a stay-at-home mother. My mom is one of the strongest women I know and realizing that she grew from this situation (and fully held my father accountable for his actions) has only made me admire her more. Where the answer might be easy for some people if that was their relationship, I honestly don't know what I would do. There's so many factors to consider. I do know that a part of me would forgive and not necessarily *hate* my partner. My father is not a bad guy. He just made *one* bad decision, and there were many factors in his life that created the environment for that fork in the road. Keeping that in mind, I would have to consider many aspects of the marriage before I make a decision based solely on emotions as life is not black and white, but shades of gray.

* *

While writing this book, I was able to have an enlightening conversation with a sorority sister of mine, Roselyn

Aker-Black, affectionately known as Dr. Roz. A clinical psychologist and relationship expert in Washington, D.C, she received her Bachelors of Arts degree in Psychology, and a Doctorate in Clinical Psychology with a focus on family, child, and forensics psychology.

Dr. Roz entered into the field of relationships when she started working at a non-profit organization, the former E Capital Center for Change, now known as LifeStart. The program's purpose initially was to stop gangs in east DC. They hired convicted felons and those who had "street credibility" to talk with the youth in the schools of East DC and run the in-school suspension program. The purpose of this was to teach kids how certain actions can impact your life in the long-term. Dr. Roz soon realized that the behavior modifications of these students were not as impactful outside of program because the children would go home and not see healthy relationships in their everyday homes. The key to creating healthy relationships starts at home.

During her career, she learned that people are not taught how to have healthy relationships. People will just begin to mirror what they see and display "default behavior," meaning they replicate and learn to relate to the world from who they initially see. This could be their parents, grandparents, and any other close peers that they subconsciously look up to during the early and middle stages of their development.

Because people aren't specifically taught how to have healthy relationships, individuals tend to go into this mode of "trial-and-error" in figuring out how to have healthy relationships based on what we see and how we learn from our errors. So, not only are we attaching what we learned from our observation of the people around us, but we then begin to tutor ourselves on how to navigate dating and relationships.

## WHAT IS A HEALTHY RELATIONSHIP?

Defined by Dr. Roz, "a healthy relationship is where individuals are functioning in an appropriate manner. There is emotional support and physical support. By physical support, I mean safety."

Emotionally, individuals must feel safe being authentic, genuine, true, and *vulnerable* in their partnership.

Physically, individuals must feel comfortable, protected, and secure.

Mentally, individuals must feel sound, engaged, and open.

Thus, there exists a synergy between healthy relationships and the healthy usage of social media.

When creating new relationships, it is important to be

cognizant of your actions and the way you navigate various platforms. . . whether this is your relationship with social media or another human being.

Are you truly your authentic self on social media? While it's okay not to reveal your complete self to strangers in the very beginning, it is important to be authentic for the sake of emotional stability. In a relationship, people may unintentionally create a falsified conception of who they are with their partner by not being their honest selves from the very beginning. One of the keys to a successful and fulfilling relationship is being able to be vulnerable and open with another person. You and your partner must create spaces where vulnerability is handled in a healthy manner. You must each take care of each other's vulnerabilities and refrain from using your partner's vulnerabilities against them.

In both the digital and physical settings, you must be prepared and comfortable with being yourself. An individual will never be able to fully attain gratification and acceptance from others if they are not being genuine; a part of them will always feel denied or hidden. On Instagram, would you feel comfortable posting a selfie without a filter? That's a form of vulnerability because you are putting yourself in a space to be open to criticism and compliments. . . you are opening yourself up to a reaction that you can't control. You must have the emotional strength to be okay knowing you put yourself out there and no matter the reaction you may receive, you know that you will be accepted for being the realest version of who you are. In a relationship, do you feel comfortable in those vulnerable spaces, as well? In the early stages of dating, are you open to both the criticism and the compliments?

Dr. Roz suggests that you should be very guarded with your vulnerability until the person has given you evidence that they will support you. Not everyone should know everything about you. When you get involved, make sure it is a solid relationship and make sure you understand the character of the person you want to be involved with. Ask yourself, "Is this person really worth the emotional investment?"

When merging your digital relationship and your romantic relationship, the same rules apply.

Physically, are you comfortable and secure? On a digital platform, do you feel safe and secure with what you're posting and revealing to the world around you? Your physical body language is important in analyzing your healthy behavior. What does your body language say when you are engaging with social media? When you're making a post, it's not healthy to feel nervous and have a physical reaction to those nerves when engaging with a digital platform. When you're creating an angry thread on Twitter or responding to trolls, it's not healthy to have uncontrollable anger and discomfort? Do you have forms of protection and boundaries in place? It's also important to create those boundaries in order to create security. Furthermore, in the age of *"How many likes did I get?"*, not receiving the expected gratification can drive someone psychologically into a place of withdrawal and isolation.

Being able to navigate one platform may directly reflect how you're navigating the other. Yes, it's gratifying to get likes, comments, followers and that acceptance on social media just as it's gratifying to get that attention from your partner. However, each platform has larger implications that will dictate how we engage with them on a long-term basis. It's important not rely on that gratification to dictate the health of that relationship. When merging social media and relationships, you must be genuine, comfortable, secure and open. Insecurities occur when you do not feel physically secure with your partner and the actions within the relationship create a space where one or both parties do not feel secure; for example, a direct message from a stranger to your significant other will cause insecurities. If you have emotional instabilities, you may have an unhealthy reaction to not receiving the attention you feel you need for your own emotional security. In any unhealthy relationship, you may begin to do things for likes instead of substance. In this comparison, you may do things for your partner that do not speak to who you are and what you stand for.

Having safe and comfortable behaviors so that you don't feel the physical need to remove yourself from a relationship will be beneficial for both you and those around you. Understanding your physical psyche will be beneficial for both you and your partner. In a partnership, feeling physically safe, comfortable, and secure are essential to having a healthy relationship. It is also important to be mindful of your mental health when engaging both digitally and physically. It's difficult to date if you are not mentally sound to be able to engage with others. In a relationship, you want to be mindful of the setting you're creating for your partner to also strive for healthy mental stability.

In having the emotional stability to be your genuine self, you create an honest and open space for those around you to do the same and understand that healthy relationships promote removing filters.

So, I conclude with the first lesson of this book:

Social media does not dictate who you are. You dictate who you are.

None of us are perfect and we are constantly learning how to build healthy relationships. It's important to remember that our new modes of communication and socializing are not what makes us human. It enhances what makes us human.

We are all navigating relationships and finding new ways to create new connections that will allow us to connect deeper than an LED screen.

The beauty of social media, today, is that we are able to reach further than we ever thought we could reach before. At the *swipe* of a screen, we can be connected.

## CHAPTER 2

# THE WAITLIST

*The most important career choice you'll make is who you marry. When it comes time to settle down, find someone who wants an equal partner.*

—SHERYL SANDBERG,
CHIEF OPERATING OFFICER, FACEBOOK

I was #49630 on the NYC waitlist of 49637. Looks pretty promising, I guess. I remember my friends telling me how long it took them to get off the waitlist. I didn't think too much of it. I created my profile and waited my turn.

Resembling a VIP list for a club, *The League* is exclusive. It's a premier online dating application marketed as a "community for aspiring power couples." When I think of aspiring power couples, I think of Beyoncé and Jay-Z. . . Kanye West and Kim Kardashian "KIMYE" . . . The Obamas!.. Bradgelina (#GoneButNeverForgotten). It's safe to say that none of these couples met each other via social media; however, it is possible that Kanye was enchanted by Kim's infamous selfies.

From the moment I created a profile, The League differentiated itself from other platforms to say it has *standards.* I was required to upload my LinkedIn profile to the account, and my résumé created the foundation for my profile.

A message immediately appeared in my inbox from a very good-looking man.

*Well, that was quick,* I thought.

Brown hair. Blue eyes. The right amount of facial hair. White. Handsome. His profile said Harvard Law School student. I remembered his face from the desktop website, but I didn't think too much of it. Having a first message within seconds made me feel good, as I'm sure it did for other people, no matter who it came from. He was my *Concierge.*

*Welcome to the League! Finally want to date someone that has their act together and shares your level of ambition? You've come to the right place!*

I read the concierge's message, explaining how The League works, it's features, and the process of getting started.

*Our drafting/selection algorithm prioritizes users who have received a VIP ticket from an existing member and users who have sent a referral link.*

Now, lucky me, I did have a referral code from a social event I attended that I knew would help me a bit. These referral links worked like coupon codes for The League application; however, instead of getting a discount on a specific item, this code elevates your ranking on the waitlist. I sent the code to the Harvard cutie concierge, as if it was a secret password to enter an exclusive event. It was only day one and I already felt as if I was a part of something of high caliber.

*The system also prioritizes users with 6 clear, high-quality photos and those with a fully filled out profile.*

I'm an Instagram phenom, so uploading the photos that showed my best qualities and a bit of personality was easy enough. I moved on to completing my profile.

NAME: Devin S.
AGE: 21
LOCATION: New York, New York

HEIGHT: 5'5"
EDUCATION: Georgetown University
PROFESSION: Project Manager, Student Worker
INTERESTS: Museums, Busboys & Poets, Amsterdam, MoMA, Concert-goer

*Done!* I replied to the cute concierge.

He responded, *Before passing you over to the Drafting Team for review, I recommend writing up a great About Me!*

This was the difficult part, right? What can I say about myself in about 100 characters or less . . . It has to be eye-catching. Humor works well. Don't forget a call to action, either. Knowing who my audience was, or assuming it was inner city college students, I put what I knew everyone could understand:

*A Short Cinnamon Dolce Latte with almond milk and extra whip looking for a Tall [fill in the blank].*

I sent a final message to cute concierge saying my About Me was complete. The next day, I was taken off the waitlist!

* *

By 9 PM, I had checked my e-mail fifty times that day, about five times per hour, and in the midst of emails from LinkedIn,

Facebook, and Georgetown organizations, I noticed one upcoming on-campus event worth my attention.

*A conversation with Amanda Bradford, CEO of The League, Tomorrow @ 10 AM!*

I immediately sent my RSVP to the hosting organization and woke up early the next morning to attend the event.

After a five-year relationship, Amanda Bradford realized there had been a shift in dating. "Yesterday, no one was on Tinder and today, five of my guy friends and five of my girlfriends are on Tinder," she expressed. One of her mentors told her that when you see a shift in the market (in this case, a technological shift), you notice a shift in consumer behavior. Online dating has transformed how people date and the types of platforms they are using to connect with other people. It's changing the dating "experience." Social media applications are changing human interaction and communication. The shift is constantly occurring and even evolving itself. Online dating was initially met with *Ugh* and *Sigh*. Ten years ago, there was a stigma surrounding building online relationships. Those that dated online were considered socially awkward or were said to have troubles meeting people in person. While there are people that do use online dating and social media to connect with people for those reasons, many people are attracted to this new *fad*. It's trendy.

When she first re-entered this new dating sphere, Bradford began what she called a "dating app bender" and began to realize all the things wrong with the current dating applications. What could she do to make these applications better and what were the qualifications of other people in the dating app industry? She compared herself to the "other CEO's" of eHarmony, Tinder, OkCupid, etc. She realized 1) they were all men and 2) most had financial backgrounds, not necessarily tech backgrounds. These characteristics, among with many others, already differentiated her from the pack.

After introducing her dating background, Bradford expressed how there had been a huge contrast in the type of people you meet in college and the type of people you meet in the "real world.". Physical settings, such as your college, work, extra-curricular organizations, function as real-life filters similar to those you use when online shopping.

For instance, *I want a dress that is red, no more than $50 and a size 4.*

When you input these filters, you are purposely browsing a setting where you are going potentially find what you are looking for. Going into the "real world" is leaving those filters behind and entering Macy's. You can't help but find 20 dresses that are either the wrong color, too expensive, and/or not your size. In the unfiltered world, it's inevitable that you're going to run into people that you are not looking for, whereas in a filtered digital platform, you have a greater probability of finding what you want.

Bradford, like many other developers, created a social platform for a niche market. LinkedIn is for professional networking, Handshake is for recruiting. . . She instantly realized that she wanted to filter the men she was finding on Tinder and other dating applications and find men that were on the same page as her.

> FILTER 1: Be ambitious
> FILTER 2: Interest in advancing their career
> FILTER 3: Looking for a successful, career-oriented lifestyle partner

The League platform created a space for people, primarily millennials, who are ambitious and intellectual—meant to describe create a dating space for people either pursuing higher education or in the corporate workforce.

The League is for *upscale* dating. The League is a filter.

I learned about the excitement of The League when it appeared on *Insecure*. One of the main characters, a career-focused, successful black woman was so excited that she got off the infamous "Waitlist" to be a part of this premier application.

She was now excited that she would meet guys that were not what TLC would call "scrubs." This scene a clear representation of how a group of career-focused single women just did not put their time and energy into dating and now find themselves reaching their thirties and wondering why they are not married with three kids yet. Furthermore, these women want that filter that will give them men that are on their level of success, ambition, and even income.

Seeing this scene and hearing about The League through that media pushed me to ask Bradford the question, "What was it like when you first realized your application now reached the mainstream?" It was as popular hearing about a tweet or Instagram likes. She then told me the story that she first realized it when she was "sleeping on her friend's couch, watching Jimmy Fallon."

Many millennials using these dating applications have different levels of usage that resemble the trendiness, accessibility, and the overall levels of usage of the games on our mobile devices. In turn, you are likely to engage with the following type of daters on dating applications.

"High-intent" daters use dating applications like gamers use Minecraft. They are serious players in this long-lasting game. They constantly update their profiles like gamers update their boards. They check the game probably more than once a day.

They take the game seriously because they want a serious outcome. Finding a partner requires more than a swipe. It's a swipe, a message, an exchange of numbers, and a meeting in hopes of further communication. These daters are likely to pay for usage and take advantage of the features that lead to a greater outcome—in this case, a relationship.

"Middle-intent" dating application usage resemble the usage of a game like 2048. It's not a game they play every day but on those days we do feel like playing it, we know it will take us some time to complete. We'll put in an effort to get to the final level but it's not a game we want to consciously think about on a daily basis. These daters want to try it out and see if they can get to 2048 today. If they are doing well, they may try to get to the next round of 4096. These daters are willing to date and jump into a relationship if it happens but it's not a conscious thought on their minds. They are probably thinking something consistent would be nice. Or, meeting new people will also be ideal on a Friday night where they have nothing else to do. A relationship would also be nice if something turns into that. These daters go with the flow and you'll find their usage of these applications at a much lower rate than the "high-intent" daters.

To "low-intent" daters, dating applications are just another application on their mobile device, like Temple Run or Solitaire. It's an application they downloaded a while ago and were really talented at it. They share their high score with everyone and loved seeing that they were slightly better than everyone else. These are the "let me see if I still got it" daters. What's the 'it' you might ask? These are the "daters" that like to know they can match with whomever they want to on Tinder. They know that if they go into the application, they could find secure a number of matches and even a couple of direct messages self-satisfying their own self-proclaimed attractiveness in the market. Dating applications are more of a confidence builder for these daters. These daters really don't want to jump into anything serious, but rather enjoy the game. They may be "flaky" to the other group of daters who genuinely want to meet and connect with other people.

Despite the general filters we can use to find potential partners (age, distance, race, background, height, interests), we can't filter intentions and the type of dater we are looking for. Statistics show that fifty-nine percent of millennials want to use online dating applications as a tool to meet new people, not to just date.

In the globally connected world, social media has inched its way into every detail of our lives, including our dating lives. While we may not directly adhere to the effects, social media has changed the way we engaged with one another and how we've represented ourselves.

People can represent themselves differently online than how they represent themselves in person. People may not look put together in person all of the time but they will get 500+ likes on a singular moment in time when they felt confident and #slayed. That singular moment is persuading people to want to engage with others. And one photo, if done right, can command the attention of all who ever your space.

As a hopeless romantic, I am here to admit that I would go sit in coffee shops just to see if a cute guy would come up to me and inquire about the book I'm pretending to read. In some of my personal stories you'll read throughout this book, I convinced myself at one point that meeting people online wasn't for me. What I learned to realize was that certain behaviors in real life mirrored behaviors on social media.

On social media, I could post a picture of a book I'm pretending to be interested in, inhibit the same false perception, and still meet a potential partner. The purpose of that book and intention of showing it off, in either scenario, is the same. It's these types of behaviors that I will analyze. Our behaviors in real life are only extended to our digital platforms. Depending on the genuine or candid behaviors we choose to portray will affect the types of relationships we engage in. And when it comes to filters, the digital arena allows people to adhere to these filters even if it's not their reality.

The League was a platform that allowed for daters to filter out the type of people they did not want to engage with. The platform inspired both men and women to engage with strangers, expand their horizons and expose themselves to a new social experience that didn't exist a decade ago. That same reason is why all social media applications have changed consumer behavior.

This social phenomenon is becoming normal.

# CHAPTER 3

# A SOCIAL PHENOMENON

*If you were the inventors of Facebook. you would've invented Facebook.*

—MARK ZUCKERBERG, *THE SOCIAL NETWORK*, 2011

* *

*'Hey, I'm your aunt.' That's what a random lady on Facebook messaged me one day.*

*I was so confused because she was like the same age as me and I had no idea who she was. It was weird. I didn't respond.*

*I immediately Facebook messaged my mom since she was*

*online. Eventually, I felt the need to connect them, especially since this lady was obviously trying to connect to the family.*

*After some searching, we found out that she was my mom's dad's other wife's daughter, my grandfather was a rolling stone, and well . . . I have a new aunt.*

Google "Facebook reunites family" and hundreds of stories are found. Seriously, google it.

* *

*How can you be social if you have to use some type of media to be social?* asked my grandfather.

He's from the "they just don't get it" generation. This was definitely followed by a "back in my time" story that I won't get into because it will take up the entire chapter. However, a few moments later, he's asking to see photos of our family on *the* Facebook.

Well, Grandpa, to answer your question, people have been using media to socialize forever.

The definition of social in this context is the interaction of the individual and the group. Media is the means of communication. The first known use of the phrase *social media* was in 2004. Coincidently, Facebook was also founded in 2004.

I joined *the* Facebook in March 2009. My first friend was my mom because she was probably next to me when I made it. My first status: *talkin to my friends ;;hearts;;*

Imagine that, kids. Facebook didn't understand emojis just yet.

I remember what it was like to find everyone on Facebook. Before that, my friends and I would use Yahoo! Messenger and even had a chain of emails that we sent to each other.

On Facebook, it was like school outside of school hours. We knew what everyone was doing afterwards and anything that happened after hours. The cliques were still talking within their respective cliques. But, it was still modest because some of us had parents watching.

Facebook was the family social network. It was where Grandma could see updated photos of me and my brothers and my aunts were loyal likers of all my posts.

It's interesting how Facebook was originally created to connect with people you already knew. It was a way for friends to stay connected after social gatherings, work, and family events. Facebook's intended purpose was to connect with people you already knew or could get to know that were in a close vicinity, such as a college campus or workplace. Today, users befriend strangers and pen pals worldwide. It's a way to connect with strangers. You meet people you don't know and friend people who are mutual friends of other people you knew from another mutual friend. Facebook created this new way of connecting people and I would say, 2004 was the beginning.

* *

"Kids Tell Their Parents How They Lost Their Virginity." These are the types of videos I click on YouTube because they show actual people communicating with one another about any topic. Couples discuss love. Opposing political views talk politics. This one began with two women—one in a red dress and the other in yellow, the strict-Asian mother and the first generation Asian-American daughter. My first thought is just how beautiful the daughter was. She was very gentle, kind and eye-catching. She was also slightly awkward, which made her stand out from the rest. Her name is Ilah. I knew that this conversation would immediately stick out to me. Her mom asked her, "when did you lose your virginity?" She responded, "When do you think I lost it?" Yep, sounds like my conversation with my parents.

The video would go on to show about five different parent and child (who are now adults) interactions discussing virginity loss. Each of the opening scenes of Ilah were a bit silent and awkward. You could tell she did not want to talk about this. She would constantly look at her mom, giggle, then look away. Then as the children are all answering the question of whether or not they used protection Ilah's scene was the most shocking. She said, "I didn't and well, I have a one year old who I love." If the camera did not pan to her mother's face, this moment would not have meant much to the audience. Like, okay she has a one-year old because she didn't use protection. Understandable. But, her mom's face looked shocked. Eyebrows raised. Jaw slightly open. Her gaze did not leave her daughter's face. She didn't blink in a span of the next thirty seconds. *Did Ilah just tell her mom she got pregnant and has a child? Was this her confession?* This left not just me (I went through the comments trying to dig for an explanation to Ilah's mother's shock), but hundreds viewers in disbelief.

In the following scene, both women are in tears. Ilah began to cry and continued to explain how her pregnancy affected her. Her mother did not even look at her nor the camera.

I thought, *What TF just happened on Youtube?*

The second video was just Ilah's interview, not compiled with other peoples. The entire awkward interaction was in one place. When watching the full video, the entire conversation made more sense, without all the video editing and cuts. Ilah did get pregnant her first time, and her mother knew that. That revelation is not what caused the emotions to break out later in the video. Obviously, her mother knew she was pregnant and had a child; however, the details of who where and how sparked that emotion from each of them.

*Guilt.* Her mother asked Ilah if she felt guilty about not being honest about when she got pregnant. Ilah felt hurt that she couldn't talk to her parents about the situation.

Now I'm invested in this beautiful stranger's story. I continued to dig through the comments to figure out who this girl is. Her story left people asking for more details because of the emotional and confusing moment she and her mother shared on camera. After about five minutes or less of digging, I found her Instagram.

One thing I realized about these types of raw videos is social media allows us to see that other people have connected with this person, post, tweet, etc. We are all similar in why we chose to engage with this stranger or retweet this tweet or love a post. As I was invested in Ilah's story, I and other strangers took to her Instagram to see her daughter that she loved, the relationship with her family, and all these details about the life of a stranger I will likely not encounter in real life. Because of her video on Youtube, I felt compassion for Ilah and wanted to support her.

In scrolling, I found a post of her and her boyfriend celebrating their anniversary. I swiped left to see the thread of what I assumed to be selfies that they've taken together over the years. The second photo in the thread of photos was not another selfie, or family photo, or a #MCM picture showing off her man. It was a screenshot of an Instagram message.

> I know this is really random. Also, now that I think of it, pretty weird. Oh, well I'm already here and I've already began typing what I need to get off my chest! 😳 After seeing the first ten seconds of the WatchCut video, I had to try and find your Instagram or something. You're seriously the most insanely gorgeous human being I've ever seen. 👽 Welp, that's all I needed to get off my chest. Didn't think I'd make it here to tell ya. 😬

The day after the video of Ilah and her mom was posted, her now boyfriend sent her the above message. She messaged him back appreciating his message. The conversation continued from Instagram to a phone call. After two weeks, they met in person.

They have now been dating for two years.

This is possible because of the social platforms that we have at our disposable, and also the human behaviors that have stemmed from these social platforms. For example, the courage and confidence that some people have gained by using these platforms have encouraged more genuine connections and more risks that are being taken.

This stranger pursued from YouTube to Instagram to let this girl, who just poured out how she lost her virginity and that she has a child, know that she is beautiful. Just as I didn't know, he did not know who she was, where she was or if he would ever meet her in person. However, today's society makes it possible to transfer a digital interaction to a physical connection. This is what dating today looks like.

What if I told you that you would find your significant other in a GroupMe group of 250 people? You go into this GroupMe, specifically looking for housing for the upcoming summer internship. You ask if anyone could help you find a place in the nearby area. Everyone points you to this one person and that person begins to message you. They're kind of attractive, but that's beyond the point. You engage in small talk to figure out your next housing spot for your upcoming internship. This is obviously something temporary. A spot opens up in this person's house (it's set up for students, nothing creepy). Next thing you know, you are in a relationship.

My friend Jen had primarily been using Tinder to date, in general. At that point, she didn't feel like she had any sustainable romantic relationships from the dates that she had been going on. She made a lot of connections, but most would just stay in the friendship level.

When she met this new guy, it was understood that it would be a hook-up; neither of them wanted a long-term committed relationship. That standard was understood from the beginning. After a month of dating, they decided together that they wanted to make the relationship official.

*He was respectful, which is sometimes missing when people are looking for hookups. He was genuine in wanting to connect. His age came with maturation that is sometimes difficult to find in dating people who are closer to my age. It genuinely felt right. He felt authentic.*

She allowed herself to get to know him beyond the superficial pieces that she usually focused on in her "hook-up" relationships.

But, what really prompted Jen to swipe right?

*His profile said 'English accent.'*

They've now been dating for more than a year and growing strong.

**This is what a "hello" today looks like. It's unconventional. It's random. It's spontaneous.**

These types of stories are not unusual to the lay social media user.

Interactions with strangers are becoming more common because we now have access to one another. Today, over 1.5 billion people worldwide have a Facebook account. Statistics say that we each know each other by a degree of 3.5, meaning we can all be connected by a third or fourth person we all know.

Less than a year ago, this number was 7.

CHAPTER 4

# RAPID REWARDS

*Our goal is to not just be a photo-sharing app, but to be the way you share your life when you're on the go.*

—KEVIN SYSTROM, CEO/FOUNDER, INSTAGRAM

If you are an active user of any social media application, you are likely addicted to social media. It's a science, actually.

Nucleus accumbens, also known as NAc, is the portion of our brain referred to as the "pleasure center" or the "reward circuit". According to the Canadian Institutes of Health Research, the NAc's operation is based chiefly on two essential neurotransmitters: dopamine, which promotes desire, and serotonin, whose effects include satiety and inhibition. It allows us to process our pleasures, including money, food, sex, and our reputations.

Positive feedback on Facebook lights up that little piece of our brain. The more we use Facebook, the more we feel rewarded with this pleasure.

You know that feeling of eating your favorite chocolate treat? The rich taste as it hits your tongue and the sweetness as it slowly melts.

Or, if you're not a chocolate person, your favorite beer. A cold beer, a Corona with lime perhaps, definitely not Natty, at a summer day party or cookout.

Chocolate and beer are processed as rewards.

Now, think about your favorite photo on Instagram. Remember when you got ready to post it? You found the best and clearest one after a series of takes that were either too blurry, not framed correctly, or something about your stance was just awkward. You found the one where the lighting hit just right. With a few edits here and there, it was finally post-worthy. So, you posted it. Moments later, you received 10 likes in a minute. 25 likes in two. 100+ in the next 10, and so on.

This is the reward.

As with many things that bring us joy, we tend to rely on them for that rewarding feeling. Getting likes and receiving comments are rewards that both touch on our care for our reputations and our distaste for loneliness.

The science is even deeper than that, though.

The first picture posted on Instagram was a picture of a dog and a foot. A dog. . . next to a foot. . . a foot in a flip-flop. The photo-sharing social media application, now owned by Facebook, has 700 million users. When it started, people were attracted to the platform because Instagram could take a regular photo and turn it into a B/W cliché, a 70's polaroid look, or just emphasize and enhance the color.

The founders of Instagram started the application because they believed "each and every person had a visual voice inside." That visual voice becomes our daily highlighted moments, best lighting selfie days, #OOTD (outfit of the day), our personal interests, and sometimes creative quotes and captions. It's a way to tell your story and personality through a visual photo.

People were attracted to Instagram for many reasons. It was different from Facebook in that it was just photos and nothing else—no long drawn out posts about who-knows-what, no "Like this post if you want to rate you," no random journal entries. It was simple and to the point. Here's a picture of XYZ that I'm proud of. And, instead of a long-written post, captions were short and sweet—a light description.

For me, it was easy to switch over to Instagram when parents began to invade Facebook. Generation X'ers were beginning to realize that social media could help them connect with their older friends and share their current lives with people they haven't kept in touch with over the years. Facebook was no longer private from the parents' gaze. Instagram was the new application that would probably take the older generation even longer to download, and they will probably not care to share photos of themselves. I don't know about your parents, but mine still take selfies from the chin up.

Millennials and post-millennials adopted Instagram instantly. The simple platform that showed the important information—followers, following, posts, and likes—kept a basic level of what people wanted to see and share. Instead of reading or digging through the liked pages or interests on Facebook, Instagram showed what people were interested in through photo-sharing. It was also a way for people to promote themselves #selfie.

Instagram also became a platform that celebrities actually felt comfortable using. It was a great way for celebrities to choose what they wanted to share and when. The posts could be a personal look at their own lives and they weren't required to engage with anyone they didn't want to engage with. Instagram was the best platform for famous people to be themselves and still hold a sense of privacy.

*They trade likes, comments, and it becomes a whole new social graph.*

We *like* photos and posts because it shows our sense of individuality, expresses who we are, and makes us relatable. We see something and it's instant gratification that we are like the others that have liked that brand or page or post. We also *like* because it's our way of literally thumbs-upping someone else's post. If it's someone we know, it's like giving your friend a fist bump or a pat on the back. If it's a stranger, it's like a nod or friendly smile when walking down the street. If it's an attractive stranger, it's a wink and maybe even a slight wave depending on your style, in hopes that that person follows your eyes until they reach you from across the room and that acknowledgment from across the room is now a "hey, what's your name?"

Consequently, Pew Researchers found that one of the top reasons we like other people's post is the hope that we get something in return, whether it be a like, comment. If it's the matter of liking a business page, we expect some type of coupon-- human nature at its finest.

Today, Instagram is one of the most active social media applications that completely fulfilled Systrom's original purpose for the platform. Post whatever you want. Follow. Comment. Like. Hashtag. Direct Message.

It's not surprising nor unusual to meet a millennial that does not utilize social media. Even I am very limited on my social media use compared to that of my friends. However, how many people (younger than 40) do you know that do not have Instagram or Snapchat? Most people in their 20s have at least one mode of social media. To be exact, a whopping 86% of U.S. adults between the ages of 18 and 29 have at least one social media account. My friend Liv is actually one of the 14%. An educated Georgetown alum with a good job, living in a single apartment with a beautiful sunset view, a good relationship, and a seemingly successful life does not have a social media to show you all of her accomplishments. Why? Simply because she does not care nor want to.

*I don't have an Instagram. It's addictive,* she says.

From her perspective, people become addicted to the number of friends they have (friends being followers who are most likely classmates, one-time conversations and strangers). They constantly trace their likes and the number of comments they have. People will follow how many people are seemingly interested in their lives because likes, comments, and DM's define the level of interest someone has in you . . . or that's how we see it sometimes. You're presenting a perceived version of your life through a feed of paused moments and short boomerang recaps of day to day moments in one's life.

*If your entire purpose is posting to have a mainstream following just to have a brand that is you then what's the point? If your purpose is to have a following for no reason other than likes, followers and DM's then what's the point?*

This is what we must decide on. There are positives and negatives to every aspect of our lives, including our social media usage and we must be cognizant of both sides. It's important to realize that social media is not an entire person but a slight perception of one's day to day, and usually the most exciting or interesting part, of someone's life.

Remember your last vacation. How many times did you take out your phone to take a picture? How many times did you pause the present to capture a single glimpse of your experience? How long did it take for you to want to post that photo immediately? Did you take that photo for yourself or for your social followers?

There's a difference between capturing a memory and searching for likes. There's a different intent and purpose.

If you're not someone that pauses the moment and experience to capture a flick #ForTheGram then I'm sure you know a friend that does do that and the feeling you get as you're waiting for them to get "the perfect photo."

As soon as we get a connection in addition to that good lighting, photos are going up.

It's as if the person only wanted to enjoy the experience in order to share the glamour with their followers and receive positive feedback of compliments and approval. They wanted to trigger a jealousy and/or admiration [by their followers] based on a perception [of their own life].

Why? The *reward* is *gratifying*. Gratification, to be clear, is a source of satisfaction or pleasure.

For my readers who know, Howard University's Homecoming is one of those events where you can search the hashtag #HUHC[InsertYear] and find a million photos of people who have attended. It's known for the "slay." You dress to impress when you go to Howard University's Homecoming, especially as an undergraduate or graduate African-American student. There are many events like this that have the same type of effect (#Coachella2018), no matter who is in attendance. According to Liv, this event was solely for the slay and depending on your crew, you either went for the excitement of meeting up with people and reconnected with former classmates and faculty or you went to get that *Insta* flick that you hoped would go rival. Well, Liv's boyfriend was a Howard alum who found that homecoming was the perfect time for his entire crew will be back to the District.

It was an interesting conversation with Liv as she told me her reservations and why she ended up not going with her boo to the homecoming festivities. Liv didn't want to go just to stand around while everyone takes Instagram photos and slay #FortheGram. She was less interested in going just because she knew how social media will "get in the way of people enjoying the moment." Contrastingly, her boyfriend didn't see it that way at all. Him and his college friends were reconnecting with each other and wanted to have a good time. Will flicks be taken? Of course. Is that the point of going? No. Unfortunately, they saw that moment differently.

Now, what about the other perspective of this exact moment? People look up those hashtags to see who is in attendance. Maybe find a prospective #BAE and enjoy the moments that millions of people are able to share. Some people are posting, not for the gratitude, but for the memory itself and to show their friends and strangers.

"Hey, I was there! Just like you." It's a way of connecting beyond our immediate circles.

When asked about his favorite photo on Instagram, Kevin Systrom claimed it wasn't what you would think his favorite photo would be. It wasn't his most-liked photo. It wasn't the best quality. It wasn't the greatest selfie Kim Kardashian would approve of. It was the photo of a dog. . . and a foot. It was a moment in time, now documented forever and for everyone beyond his immediate circle to see.

## CHAPTER 5

# SUBTWEET

*If you don't have a goal, a purpose for your relationship, or pretty much anything, if you don't have a place for anything, something you want to accomplish, something you want to do, you can really get lost in the murk of the journey.*

—WILL AND JADA PINKETT-SMITH

*I've gotten to the point where I can watch his snap story and my heart not fall to my butt.* That's a direct quote from a close friend re-encountering her last "situationship."

Remember those iMessage games, GamePigeon, that everyone was playing? There was Connect4, Pool, Basketball, etc. Eric tweeted something about if anyone to play those iMessage games and she was really bored at the moment. After analyzing his profile, realizing he was cute enough to receive her number, Jade slid in his DMs. Eric responded immediately, they exchanged numbers and this began the one-on-one tournament of Connect 4.

It was the beginning of December. They played those games for a while. Trash-talking slowly turned into small talk, small-talk turned into more meaningful conversation. Where are you from? Where are you going? What are your goals? What was your childhood like? Tell me about your parents. You know, all those 21 Questions type of details.

Soon, they even discussed going on a date... Let's just say that plan fell through. From texts and talking to him on Facetime, Jade concluded that when Eric thinks people are mad at him, he retreats. However, being ignored made Jade even more mad about the failing date situation. So, of course, Jade turned to Twitter to tweet her feelings about not talking to somebody. He obviously caught the subtweet and messaged her about the failed date. Even though their texts and his tweets weren't adding up, she gave him a chance to make it up to her.

They Facetime'd a lot... all through Christmas break and into the new year. They hadn't talked about super serious things but he had seen her in a very comfortable state—sweatpants, hair-tied, chilling with no make up on type of thing.

Her mom had a lot of reservations about her liking and

starting to talk to a guy via internet. She just wanted to make sure her daughter was safe, and she knew she should be careful, too. She made sure to have precautions and not jump into something too soon.

They finally went on their first date! They went to the movies, talked, walked together and went back to her apartment. There was some kissing, ya' know. And, that was end of the night. It was great, supposedly.

Now it's near the end of January. They Facetime'd some more; it was their main form of communication. The next time they hung out again at his house.

They kissed . . . a lot. At this point in the relationship, she figured it'd be good to talk about the future of the relationships. The conversation was going well, but then all of sudden, things changed. Eric just kept talking about him going to college and feeling like he wouldn't want to be faithful. She told him they could just talk and be friends, since they obviously didn't want the same things romantically, especially since one person thought it would go nowhere. She was honestly just confused because he wasn't even giving her a chance. Was that too much to ask for? If you like someone enough, you'd do that for them. He asked if she was okay with her decision. She said it is what it is. After that, she didn't hear from him at all.

This isn't an unusual encounter. The reason dating may not get past the "talking" stage is because there's a lack of communication on what the expectations are and a lack of communication on which direction the relationship is going. What are your expectations for the relationship? Many people are scared to ask the goals of the relationship, the hard questions, the "Defining the relationship" (DTR) conversation. What's confusing is that people will dive in without understanding the other person's final goal. Let's say I never wanted to date and just wanted to have a casual sex type of relationship. It's not until six months later that person wants to know what you wanted, and you both realize those goals are not the same. Would you ever enter into a contract without understanding the final goal? What if you and the other party have differing goals? You may not have ever wanted what the other party wanted.

As we engage in social media more, research shows that the view on engaging in sex is changing as well. As a generation, millennials are more comfortable having sex and being cuddled up during the earlier dates. However, there is a fear of asking a partner the expectations of the relationship. It's pretty backwards. Communication and understanding what expectations are backwards; nothing should come as a surprise. The more two people communicate and the better they communicate, as uncomfortable as it is, the better off they are.

Is the key to communication that communication is key? What I've learned over time is that one of the causes of issues that people face in general stem from a miscommunication somewhere down the line.

One of the most difficult and uncomfortable conversations that are needed in relationships starts at "This is what I'm expecting and you're not living up to it." Unfortunately, some of us may be more likely to tweet it than actually say it.

* *

Originally imagined as a text message-based communication platform, Twitter, founded in 2006 by Jack Dorsey, is a global social media platform used for public self-expression and conversation in real time. It is now worth $32.9 billion and has over 328 million active users.

It's mission, to "give everyone the power to create and share ideas and information instantly, without barriers," fully encompasses how its active users constantly engage with the platform on a daily basis. Twitter is used by many to share their raw and genuine thoughts, feelings, and statuses in a short, limited version. On Twitter, everyone has a voice.

It differentiated from Facebook in that Twitter was created to be quick notifications to your friends about what you are doing and where you are in real-time. Let your friends know you're at 230 Fifth Ave in New York City and hope they can meet you there.

When you were feeling inspirational, you could tweet a quote, lyric, or original content. Pro tip: Anything about heartbreak, love, and sex will likely get a lot of retweets whether people can relate to it or not because everyone feels like a romance expert on this platform.

As an avid Twitter user for almost 8 years, I can note that this platform transformed the way millennials and post-millennials communicated with each other with 140 characters or less.

The content is random, current and up-to-date. Twitter is noted to have originated the platform of highlighting trending topics and hashtags and then analyze the conversations regarding either of those links. If you are trending, the algorithm concludes you have received on average, depending on the time you are tweeting, 1500 tweets regarding your topic, at least 600 different users discussing your topic and the number of impressions you receive (retweets, mentions, likes).

The birth of the hashtag changed the way people engage in conversation. Between #relationshipgoals #Bae #HeGonnaMissMeWhenImGone, hashtags became the new way to highlight the important headlines of a posts, reaction or phrasing.

If any of you wondered if your friends would prefer a like or a comment on a post, science says comment. Based on her research of more than 1000 Facebook users, Moira Burke, computational social psychologist at Facebook stated, "People who received composed communication became less lonely, while people who received one-click communication experienced no change in loneliness." It's simple. People like conversation, which explains why Twitter was also very successful.

> *I jumped in your DMs a year ago and I'm glad you were placed in my life.*—Twitter user, going on 2 years in relationship

> *In 2011 I just dropped my number in her DM & hoped for the best. Now approaching 6 years together and 2 years of marriage #WeMetOnTwitter*—Twitter User

> *@XXXXXX waiting on a follow back*—Twitter user, now married for 6 years

For some, it started with a DM—an eye emoji, heart eyes, "Wyd up this late" text, "Let me shoot my shot" messages, and a variation of many others that leave many people today engaging with each other online and having the confidence to reach out to their crush.

When you hear about, see, or think Twitter, dating may not be the first thing to come to mind, and this is true. Twitter is not a dating platform and not designed to be that. However, Twitter connects people beyond selfies. It connects conversations and people's daily thoughts. You share your interests with others and others engage in conversation. This is the platform created to enhance our communication and daily conversation values. When looking at someone's Twitter, while you do see what they look like, you pay attention to their tweets and what they are saying.

As Twitter engages us with the world and when you are able to understand the thoughts and interests of a person based on their own voice, who's to say it isn't a platform where you can find potential partners.

Kiran David, 23, is what most would deem as "Twitter famous." He's a peer of mine, a millennial. It's interesting how someone like him has created their signal foundation on a social media platform and has since published two books and continues to speak to people on faith, love, and now his music. From London, but having an avid relocation history, like myself, this now Bay area resident has revolutionized how we tell stories on Twitter and creating stories that connect people from around the world. Now, how does Kiran relate to my book and my stories? He's an unconventional expert on relationships because he has learned to understand people in his own relationship experience. But Kiran's contribution is double-faceted. Not only does he have those relationship stories, but he also understands how social media can work to his benefit.

> When it comes to Twitter, **timing is everything**. I genuinely feel like the advice I gave wasn't revolutionary in its meaning. But, it was revolutionary in its **presentation** and timing. It's all about who sees your stuff and when. You can have the best idea or the advice but if you don't post it at the right time or say it the right way, it's not going to reach the same [magnitude].

His thread has now reached over 50,000 people on Twitter and even more since articles were released and his own publications about the thread. "The Indecisive Perfect Guy," its title, detailed a type of guy that I would say is a majority of the adolescent males that I've been in contact with.

> *You meet this guy via Twitter or life or whatever... Seems cool enough. Not sexy, not ugly. But attractive... Carries himself well.*

The exchange I had with Kiran regarding the thread gave insight into the male perspective and how women play the game of relationships and just how our generation begins to deal with a different set of issues that has stemmed from our access to each other. **While our modes of communication have changed, people have not.** The "Indecisive Perfect Guy" is that guy that had all the potential to be a girl's next step but then a key piece of communicating that next step went missing along the way.

> *Ya'll start talking and the vibe is DOPE. Like ya'll connect. Convo flows. He's really easy to talk to. Texts back timely. The whole 9.*
>
> *Ya'll go out. He's amazing. You have a great time. Perfect gentleman. Everything is lit. Ya'll go out again. More of the same.*

If everything is going great, how does the guy get the label "indecisive"?

> *You text one day and he replies slower than usual... JUST... Slow enough where you can tell something is off with you two's energy...*
>
> *He doesn't call as often.. He's not as hyped to talk to you. He still likes you you know. But you can feel this sense of doubt on him...*

From the other side's standpoint, this is the switch-up. The guy is all of a sudden "uninterested" and that un-interest stems randomly. As time goes on, you both just tend to fall off, and if you're on the confused end of this interaction, you move on but contemplate where you went wrong. . .

The "situationship" some of us experience is all tied back to our communication and our fear of communicating what we actually want from another person. It's ironic how in this day and age, we are the most connected generation. Our communication is constant and there's a want and a subconscious need for constant communication. We have the tools to be the most communicative generation, and yet it appears sometimes that we don't use them the right way. It's the greatest strength and the greatest weakness.

It's easier to subtweet (talk about someone in a tweet without actually saying it to them directly or mentioning them indirectly) than to tell someone what you actually want to say. Fortunately, Twitter gives people a sense of comfort and honesty. It's the platform that shares our words, and because the context is limited, we are able to say more with less. It's not at all that we are bad communicators, but we use indirect methods. Has this really ever changed, though?

Shakespeare could not have been any clearer about miscommunication in his most famous love story:

> @ROMEO: *What light through yonder window breaks?. . . It is my lady; O, it is my love! O, that she knew she were!* (83 characters)

> @JULIET: *Or, if thou wilt not, be but sworn my love, And I'll no longer be a Capulet.* (60 characters)

Unfortunately, for those of us that remember Act 2, Scene 2 . . . the famous aside, although said in near proximity, were not heard by the other.

## CHAPTER 6

# TRIPLE DIGITS

*The number one indicator or signal that you will [live to] make it to triple digits [100 years old]: How many people do you love?*

—SCOTT GALLOWAY, PROFESSOR OF MARKETING, NYU STERN SCHOOL OF BUSINESS

As the usage of social media evolved, so did Facebook's stated mission and purpose.

In 2004, the mission of *The* Facebook was to connect people through social networks at colleges. The platform was exclusive to college students, first at Harvard, and then expanded to other colleges, as well.

As the platform experienced growth and much popularity among early adopters of social platforms, and MySpace began to lose traction, *The* Facebook became *an online directory that connects people through social networks at schools.* Over time, it transformed from connecting with people at your own school, to now all schools, to the "people around you" to "people in your life."

The platforms that created the most connections are now the most successful. Facebook in 2017 has reached over 2 billion monthly active users, and trust me that it is not because of its sleek look, marketing techniques, or because it's measurably *better* than all the other platforms. Until June of 2017, Facebook's mission fulfilled what it meant to be a platform that connects human to human:

> *To give people the power to share and make the world more open and connected*

The most successful dating applications are not the applications that have the most marriages, the most long-term relationships, and the other metrics that sites like Match.com and OkCupid use to market themselves. At the end of the day, this data is immeasurable. While these platforms can say they lead to more marriages and more dates, they are not the reason the man got down on one knee and the woman started to look for the *perfect* wedding dress. That's a product of the relationship, not Match.

What these platforms should say in their marketing is *Hey, we are XYZ, and we lead to the most Hellos.*

* *

Betty, 61, was single and ready to mingle in her later years. She didn't have a husband in the picture, and children were grown and out of the house. She lived in Manhattan, and financially sound. She decided to use Match to get back out there and possibly find that partner that she could spend the rest of her life with . . . Betty would exclaim that you're never too old to find a partner.

Betty got on Match and paid for someone to do her profile for her. She didn't know exactly what to do, so she paid somebody to figure it out for her. That consultant told her which photos would give her the best profile responses, how much information to put in her biography and the different interests that would spark the interests of others and give her a good quantity of quality responders. In no time, Betty got her first match, and in turn, a first date.

Richard was a very educated man. He was in the same age range as Betty and a principal of a school. Betty liked Richard. For one, he was handsome, offered good conversation and the dates were fun for the most part. The first date led to many more afterwards. As time went on, Betty and Richard reached a level of intimacy. . . physical intimacy. Betty enjoyed that too. However, overtime Richard admitted, "I use a pump." Betty was confused as to what was going on and why Richard was saying this. She responded, "What's a pump?" It was pump used by men who have erectile dysfunction. . . That was the last time Betty saw Richard.

The second date was an actor named Clarence from Washington D.C. Betty learned that he was planning to move to NY and could see the potential in this guy. They had an undeniable chemistry. Betty opened up to her friends that she was ready to get intimate with Clarence, but before they could get intimate, she wanted to check if he had STDs or STIs. . . specifically, AIDS. She was in her 60s so given the times she grew up in and the STD that people specifically worried about was AIDS. You could not convince Betty that any other sexually transmitted diseases existed that she may want to check. Betty went on and on to her friends that really hoped Clarence did not have AIDS. Fortunately, they got cleared and both were ready to get intimate. A few weeks later, Betty came back to her friends and told them, "This is not what I signed up for." They ended up being incompatible.

The third guy was a successful CEO. Let's call him Thomas. He was retired, wealthy, lived in an upscale gated community, drove a luxury car and everything about him was wonderful. "But he was too fat. His belly was too big," exclaimed

Betty. However, she gave him a chance. Thomas was very worldly, and he took her to nice places. Betty was wined and dined. They dated for a while, to the point where she went to his house often, and Betty would go on and on about how "it was very nice." The house was nice . . . Thomas was okay . . . But, Betty did grow to like him. Unfortunately, problems occurred due to the fact that she was still working and he was retired. She wanted the relationship, but she also wanted her space. Thomas wanted more from her because he had the time. Thomas wanted someone who will go on vacations with, hang around the house, and do leisure activities. Betty wasn't going to leave her job and honestly, she just did not want to commit to that much at this point in her life. That was the end for Thomas.

That wasn't the end of using Match for Betty though. She still has many more prospective dates to get through. Betty is the *shopper* we all start out as when we decide we want to look at the market. We are open to the possibility more than anything else. It's in the beginning of our use of these platforms that we are the most open to any hellos we receive.

* *

As I was scrolling on Twitter, I noticed the hashtag #WhatsBetterThanSex.

*Yeah sex is cool but have you ever woken up before your alarm went off and realized you can sleep an extra hour*

*Yeah sex is cool but have you ever taken your bra off after a long day... (Guys, the equivalent might be anything constricting your you-know-what)*

*Yeah sex is cool but have your friends cancelled plans when you really didn't want to go out in the first place*

Yeah sex is cool but have you ever matched with the hottest person you swiped right on? This is definitely one of the best modern feelings that only today's generations will understand completely. It's a part of the game. You swipe right on somebody, and you see that "It's a Match!" Before the swiping sensations, Match.com and other online sites dominated the online dating market. They were for mature audiences, an early entrant, and successful within their targeted market segment. These platforms' unique competency was that they were able to connect people who would not otherwise be connected in real life due to time, distance, expectations, or preference.

Today, the easy right and left swipes have become the most convenient system for on-the-move millennials and post-millennials.

The idea of the swipe came about from Badeen, the tech guru of the Tinder partnership. Unfortunately, there's no exciting story to how this design came about. As a matter of fact, his inspiration could've happened to anybody. If you enjoy hot showers, you know what it's like to get out the shower, look in the mirror and wipe the mirror to admire yourself. . . About five minutes later, the mirror is foggy again . . . You wipe it again. . . Do you see the pattern here? You wipe. It resets. You wipe again. . .

You keep wiping, or swiping until something magical happens—the magic being a match.

Online dating met mobile phone game in 2012 when Tinder launched and evolved *dating* for the new generation of daters.

Tinder users swipe more than 1 billion times a day, globally. . .

It has accumulated over 20 billion friendships, relationships and even marriages since its founding.

The story of how the first two founders of Tinder came to be a partnership is essentially a match made in heaven. The two met in class and they were inseparable ever since (until recently if you're updated on the co-founder drama). They ditched their individual plans and merged into one entity. I guess you could say it was dollar signs at first sight.

Sean Rad, one of the first two co-founders of Tinder, reclaimed a day when he saw a girl in a coffee shop and that moment when you don't know whether or not to approach someone occurred. They're making eye-contact with you. You're making eye-contact with them. Eventually, some force pushes you or the other person to make the first hey, what's up, hello. Rad states, "If you can eliminate the question of whether or not someone wants to meet you, you will immediately take away the barriers of making a connection." There's no data on whether or not that girl became someone significant in Rad's life, but I'm sure she's pretty upset that she could've been a partner to one of the top application creators and social dating revolutionaries of the modern age.

From the beginning, Tinder answered the question of interests for college students. The key to this application is that,

1. You are seeing people that are actually available to you both relationship wise and location wise. These were realistic matches.
2. You know someone is genuinely interested in you because it was a match. Friends who had secret crushes or just people who never admitted interests in people are now being validated if the other person is reciprocating that interests.

Some people say Tinder has only reinforced the superficial and shallow sides of dating where people fall solely on looks to determine if someone is a good match for them or not. However, as per our biology, we're designed to have initial impressions of everyone we meet within the first ten seconds of interacting with them. However, Tinder only reinforces our innate nature to judge a book by its cover. When Rad saw that girl in the coffee shop, I'm sure his first impression wasn't her innocence, lack thereof, or anything of depth because he didn't know her. He thought she *looked* cute.

Jonathan Badeen, Tinder co-founder, stated, "Finding and selecting the appropriate button felt deliberate and sluggish, whereas in a real-world scenario, the decisions we make are quick, subconscious." Typically one's attraction is based on a person's preferences and people generally know what type of person they are attracted to physically, mentally, spiritually and emotionally. Psychology experts say it only takes seven seconds OR LESS for people to make an impression on someone, whether it be a job candidate or potential romantic partner. Tinder takes this first impression we have on others and turns it into a realistic game with realistic expectations.

**Laughs* Devin, you actually read people's Tinder profiles?*

I was confused by this remark by a couple of my guy friends. During my time abroad in Europe, myself and many of my co-travelers and classmates actually utilized Tinder, not to hook up necessarily, but to genuinely meet locals of the cities we frequented so that they could show us around the city. It was more of a way to meet people than the interest in dating. However, if a cute Spanish man found me and decided to take me on his *moto* to show me around Barceloneta, I wouldn't complain.

But, that's when I noticed the innate nature between men and women on an app like Tinder. And to be honest, I was a bit disappointed. So, guys aren't swiping right on me because they think I'm a great girl with a cool personality or corny sense of humor? How disappointing.

*Yes, Dev, guys are only swiping right on you because your first photo is you in a bikini.*

When I'm swiping on Tinder, while yes, it is a game, there is also the possibility of a true connection. So, I look at every photo and read the biographies. You'd be surprised how many guys get a swipe right because they *seem* like they have a good personality. That gives points to the lack of Odell Beckham looks in my book.

I peeked up from swiping for a second and realized my guy friends were swiping like crazy. I mean at least 100 swipes per minute. And to make matters even worse, they were swiping right on 98 of those 100 swipes per minute. It was ridiculous. My guy friends didn't care about who the girl was or if she was even super cute or nice or whatever. They swiped right if in the first few seconds if they wanted to smash and it didn't take much for them to do so.

I was appalled, but it was a bit of a reality check. It's not the apps that create these false expectations. It's the people. I was talking to a guy about social media applications at a networking event, and he said something I wouldn't forget.

*You can create all the filters you want. You can't filter out jerks and a**holes.*

Guys and girls alike, there will be people on these platforms that create dubious experiences for people who genuinely want to meet interesting people. And, it's not to say my guy friends are jerks or assholes. However, you will run into people that do not share the same expectations as you do, but that shouldn't prevent you from creating genuine experiences on these platforms.

It's unfortunate that Tinder received this reputation of being a hook-up application because what Tinder does is connect one person to someone whom they have some type of shared interest, whether it be physical or something else. It's the people, then, that can decide what they do with that match and that has nothing to do with Tinder's platform.

As previously stated in earlier chapters, back in '04 online dating was not seen as the trendy way of meeting new people, as it is today. Yet today, people still don't want to admit they met their 2-year boyfriend on Tinder and practically swiped right in order to hook-up with him, but he actually ended up being *a good one.* In 2004, most people assumed online daters were weird or awkward. In reality, most were just people who felt they didn't have time to go out and wait for the right person to walk by or they were recently divorced and trying to figure out the new dating scene.

Online dating is more efficient because of the connections it created. You are able to meet more women and men, some of a higher quality, compared to the prospective dating candidates you would meet on a daily basis. You could set up more dates in a week and filter through more matches. If anyone would have told men and women years ago that they could find a potential spouse by just sitting on their couch, they wouldn't have believed it. Yet, now their grandchildren are utilizing this approach every day.

Tinder is efficient when you realize you have thousands of options at the swipe of your phone screen. The platform's success is simply based on the fact that you can physically see more people and make more meaningful connections if you so choose.

With social media and the tools that allow you to meet as many people as you desire to, I must ask. . . how many people do you love?

Maybe not emotionally or personally, but how many people do you feel connected to on a daily basis? How many people have your interest? Your attention?

The digital world is just as important to our humanity as the real world.

We are naturally more open-minded when we open these applications on our phones. With Facebook, we are more likely to friend someone we would never speak to walking down the halls of our high schools or connect with our college peers that we've only seen around every now and then. With Match, we are more likely to date in our late 60's because it's possible. With Tinder, we learn that whether you want to admit it or not, we are judging every book by its cover. (You probably judged this book by its cover, too.) However, we are more likely to swipe right digitally on someone that we may swipe left on in real life. Each swipe, post, follow, like, and DM is a new opportunity to connect and *love* the people around us.

Each swipe right is a hello.

CHAPTER 7

# #IRL (IN REAL LIFE)

*The germ of every Meetup and all this good stuff that comes out of it is the opportunity to say 'Hello.'*

—SCOTT HEIFERMAN, CEO/FOUNDER, MEETUP

* *

@Joe1234 is now following you.

He was cute . . . in some photos. Some were definitely better than others. A few different angles are represented here. Here's his left side. Here's a full body. He looks pretty tall. He doesn't smile much, but this grin he's got going on is kind of cute.

@Joe1234 liked your photo.
@Joe1234 liked your photo.

@Joe1234 liked your photo.
@Joe1234 liked your photo.
@Joe1234 liked your photo.
@Joe1234 liked your photo.
@Joe1234 liked your photo.

Okay, so obviously he was interested in getting my attention, right? He was cute. He was located 20 minutes away. He seemed interesting.

What do you do when someone likes several of your photos at one time?

A. Follow back
B. Like several of their photos back
C. Slide in the DMs
D. Ignore and go about your day
E. Look at their profile, determine if you're actually interested and then proceed with A, B, or C.

It's easier to answer if their profile isn't private, because if it is, likely the answer is D. I rarely, if ever, go with C. I would choose B, but several photos are a lot. Maybe I'll like one or two. In this case, I decided to go with E and proceeded with A.

He sent me a direct message. He asked me how I was doing, complimented my look and my photos. He even asked about a specific photo on my Instagram that showed that I was interested in music. I liked that he was actually paying attention. Guys I talked to at the time didn't usually do that. We started talking about music and engaging in small talk.

> Where are you from? *Harlem, NY*
>
> Age? *20*
>
> What do you like to do? *I make music.*

I didn't usually want to respond to someone I met on Instagram. I'm more "old-school." I strongly believe that in person connection is truly felt when you meet a person. I always wondered, how can you really know if you're attracted to a person without seeing them in person?

So, we agreed to meet up in person, in Harlem at a fast-food restaurant. It was very casual, and appropriate for the first meeting with someone that I initially met online. I didn't know what to expect. Will he be short? Will he have a tooth missing? Is he actually who he says he is? Do I need my pepper-spray? (I always bring the pepper-spray.)

From the moment I saw him, I was ready to leave.

He looked like his photos, talked like how he did over the phone, nor did he lie about anything. I just naturally was not attracted to him. I left in about thirty minutes. He didn't have a tooth missing, but one of his teeth really did bother me.

* *

In a world surrounded by photo-sharing, looks matter. They do... but only to you. Beauty is truly in the eye of the beholder, meaning it is objective. Looks matter because we all have preferences. This is where physical attraction comes into play. The only person that needs to be attracted to your partner is you.

However, that day, I learned a key lesson to attraction:

You are either attracted to someone or you're not. You can't force it.

When Damona met her husband, of now 10 years, she was instantly attracted to his pictures, but he was not at all what she expected when she met him in person. He was "the nice guy" she knew she wanted.

Essentially, isn't that who we are all trying to find? The nice guy or the good girl are the people we want to take home to our families. And, why must we feel that there must be a compromise to get what we want?

How many times have you heard your friends say, "He's

the type of guy I should be dating, but I'm really not interested in him"? Or, "he's perfect in every way, but something is missing"?

Well, finding someone you genuinely are attracted to does not have to be a compromise. We each have our preferences for who we want, our filters, and most of the time, a relationship is a time game. When you find yourself in the right space, as an individual, whether that means financially, mentally, physically or all of the above, you will know when you are ready to bring another individual into your space.

Your eyes are dilating. You're sweating... somewhere. You're imitating movements. Your nucleus accumbens is aroused. Maybe, you're aroused?

You are feeling attracted to someone. The eyes are our greatest weapon in the laws of attraction, as well as our weakest link. The eyes give away what we're feeling, whether we realize it or not.

It's safe to say when I met up with Joe1234 in Harlem, my eyes didn't dilate.

When I met my current partner, my eyes were intensely dilating.

When my friend Christina sees a tall guy, with dark hair, on his head and face, a bit muscular but not a gym-rat, slightly tan, broad shoulders, big hands, likely on a beach or somewhere in nature . . . her eyes dilate . . . every time.

* *

I always stop and talk to Marva before I go into the student worker area. It gives me an extra ten minutes or so to gather myself before I sit and wait for work instruction. Marva is a giggly, outspoken 60 year old Caribbean lady who will never run out of things to talk about. Her personality is honestly what awarded her the front desk advisor job. She comes into work everyday, ready to leave by 4 PM. She's just your typical desk assistant with big glasses that cover a majority of her face and a bright lipstick to match her outfit. She doesn't really help you with what you asked, but she's so kind that you don't even get annoyed waiting for 10 minutes for her to call someone to answer your initial question.

"This was the first time in three decades that I'm on my own," she told me.

Marva is a widow—married for 30 years and now widowed for six. Her husband died after becoming very sick and in that moment she was left with a void in her life. Marva claims she never felt lonely but things were different. "I was at a lost.

I was grieving. After having somebody always with me, I'm now on my phone." In that moment, something in my mind clicked. This story wasn't going to solely be about a widow experiencing loss. This story is about reconnecting. Here is this 60 year old woman telling me that she found herself being more connected to the digital world after her husband passed away. That sentence—so simple in nature—symbolized the importance of the social digital world. It is in our human nature to want relationships with other people—it is communication that keeps us stable, grounded, and basically human. And, more importantly, we were meant to interact physically, not digitally.

Think about your friends who finally get into a relationship or begin consistently "dating" someone. What happens? They go ghost. They are constantly with their significant other. They don't text you back because they're with that person that releases their natural hormones. Some refer to it as lust; others refer to this feeling as cathexis. The extent of their social media usage is posting to the world that they're still in a relationship and at least one of these photos or videos is #RelationshipGoals. Now think about what happens when your friends get out of a relationship. Their social media usage increases.

No matter how much we turn to the digital world for social media engagement and interaction, the final goal in these interactions are to have physical engage with the people we meet online. That's what makes us human. Now, what does a sixty-year old widow have to do with this topic? Marva is recreating her social experience and due to the resources in this digital age, Marva is able to engage "like a millennial." She is reconnecting.

"I remember I used to tell my friends I missed 'not belonging' to someone," she continues. "Practically all my life, I was someone's wife. There's times I love my freedom, my own room, I go where I want, do what I want. But, there are times it would be nice to have a companion. It's not sexual, it's just someone to hang out with."

Marva surprised me when she described how she used Meetup, an online social networking service that allows users to organize or join offline group meetings in various localities around the world. She and her friends, group of 60+ year old women, utilized Meetup to meet new people. Is anyone else surprised by this? This is what reconnecting is. The need for social interaction transcends age and other social demographics.

Marva was surprised that she could shop for men like she shops for clothes. Cackling in between each word, she said, "You get to look and pick... Imagine that... You get to choose from a catalog of dates. Who would've thought?" I wondered if she was giggling at this because of her youth. More than a decade ago, people actually had to meet dates in person. Is it weird that we look at people online and decide from their profiles whether or not we're interested in them? Or, is Marva laughing because this surprisingly makes life and dating so much easier? We get a behind the scenes glimpse of people via their social online presence. It's literally window-shopping. We have different stores we can visit (Snapchat, Instagram, etc.), and some of these are specifically styled for certain people. Marva may look through an Ann Taylor before a Forever21. She is a perfect example of how the older generations of daters react to this new phenomenon of online dating.

While Marva may not be one to enter the dating scene soon, she is completely open to utilizing these new modes of social media to reconnect with men, while continuing to live her single life. It's not even about finding a husband or a long-term partner. Remember, Marva isn't lonely. She is simply reconnecting.

* *

Meetup has well over 32 million members and over hundreds of thousands meet-ups happening globally every month. It's a social platform that promotes getting off the computer and meeting up with the people offline that you find online.

An employee coup dedicated to changing the way Meetup operated sparked the question, "What if cool people were on Meetup?"

Now, when they said they wanted *cool* people, I'm confident they meant young and trendy. Marva and her friends were just a bonus to this new organizational culture. The company needed a change because the platform's users included chess enthusiasts, gaming addicts, and pet lovers.

Scott Heiferman, 44, founded the company with a mission to create these communities for everyone. The structure resembles the stereotypical cliques in a high-school cafeteria. Digitally, you can meet whichever demographic or interests that you are looking for. There are actual groups you can join and engage with offline.

Heiferman thought of Meetup after the 9/11 terrorist attacks. Living in Lower Manhattan, he met and talked to his neighbors recently after the attacks. He recalled that he engaged in more conversations with his neighbors post-9/11 than prior to the attacks. This tragedy sparked more engagement and human connection because people were reminded of an important piece of our humanity—interaction.

Meetup is specifically tailored for you to find exactly what types of groups you're looking for. Heiferman describes it as a place "for people to self-organize with other people." It's core competency was the ability to create groups. They wanted people to be a part of something bigger than themselves, or at least feel that way. However, people don't just want groups.

They want new and trendy. They want places to go. Instead of finding the who, Meetup redesigned itself to find the where.

*Where can I go to meet people who share the same interests I do?*

In the dating world, Meetup is one of the top sites to find singles looking to meet and mingle. It attracts people who want to find singles and date, but aren't ready for eHarmony. A host creates a mixer tailored for singles to meet other singles within a 25-mile radius.

On Meetup, you have RSVP lists at your access, people's profiles, their interests, and events have attended in the past and plan to attend in the future. It makes the person seem more real. Their profile isn't just saying who they are. It's saying where they go. The platform allows *daters* to really see what a person enjoys spending their time doing because they have the proof that they actually did it.

If you're interested in utilizing Meetup for dating, go for it! Create a lasting connection sparked from an initial physical meeting.

First, don't think of these events as dating. You're not going to these events to find a date. You're going to find people who you can share an experience with. You're actively doing activities that are fun and that you enjoy.

Second, be ready to socialize. As someone with an extroverted personality, I'm a firm believer in that you need to go out and socialize in order to meet *the one*. As you increase your presence outside of your home, you're more inclined to learn how to navigate social situations and converse with strangers in person. I'd encourage people who are more introverted to attempt a Meetup like setting because you will be in a space with people that share certain interests of yours and that will immediately spark conversation.

Finally, remember that the strongest relationships aren't forced. When you engage with sites created for dating, it's easy to feel like you're forcing yourself to find a relationship. As a digital platform that strives to have people use less technology and more in person communication, Meetup connects people organically. There's a physical feeling you get when you see someone you're attracted to in person versus when you find them online. Furthermore, you're putting yourself out there to be open to meeting new friends and potential dates. You're increasing your chances of meeting someone you like and not forcing a romantic engagement.

# CHAPTER 8

# SEX(TING)

*The best predictor of whether we are happy or not is our social relationships.*

—MEIK WIKING, CEO,
HAPPINESS RESEARCH INSTITUTE, COPENHAGEN

Hygge recently became my new favorite topic, and no, it's not a nickname for hygiene. Hygge, pronounced *hoo-gah* is the secret to why the Denmark is happiest place on earth, over Disney World. It's a way of life that promotes what it means to be happy and give happiness to others. It's about creating an atmosphere of coziness, and comfort where people can emit the most happiness. It's an experience rather than an object.

*Let's try hygge in the bedroom.*

One American couple thought it may be worth it to bring the tools that create the most hygge to their sex life.

*First, light candles. Hygge is not complete without candles. Danes burn about thirteen pounds of candle wax each year. It's more than you think and they tend to burn more than five candles at a time.*

Mistakenly, the couple picked a scent that didn't quite put them in the mood. Instead, the room smelled of horses, somehow, and they were soon replaced by electronic candles that had very little battery power left.

*Second, get warm and cozy. Although hygge is much more than coziness, that's how the word translates in English. The Danes are all about being comfortable. Grab a few cozy throw blankets, a scarf, definitely more than one layer, and snuggle up on a rainy night. That's the Danish hygge way.*

The couple may have overdone it. The girl was a bit overclothed for the event of the evening that would soon transpire. Additionally, searching for these layers of comfy clothes and blankets, caused a pile of clothes in the middle of the floor. With the lack of light in the room, due to the hygge standards of low lighting, both tripped at least twice trying to find their way back to bed. Eventually, after snuggling for a bit, they gently removed their layers from each other's bodies. The night was beginning to be quite *hyggelig* (translation: hygge-like, another way of saying good, nice, happy, etc.).

*Third, comfort foods. The Danes love meats, pastries and coffee. On average, they eat twice as many sweets as the regular European. Cakes are great, stews are comfortable. Popcorn is delicious, always. Hot chocolate is always an added bonus.*

The couple decided on pancakes. They are a comfort food, sweet with the drizzle of syrup on top, fluffy, and the moisture created by the melted butter on top is the best part. Pancakes can add a little spice to the bedroom, until the syrup was just a bit too sticky in the wrong places.

*Finally, cuddling. Getting cozy up next to your lover, touching, hugging, kissing, and all the things that get the mood just right.*

As soon as couple was cozied up next to each other, ready for their hygge sex... they fell asleep.

Although *hygge* in the bedroom didn't quite work out for this couple, sex is one of the greatest activities that bring people the most happiness. Meik Wiking, the CEO of the Happiness Research Institute in Copenhagen, concludes that one of the most important factors to someone's happiness is their physical encounters with other people. When we hug, touch, be near another, kiss, we feel hygge, meaning we feel happiness.

The "love drug" (oxytocin) is released in our brains and we instantly feel calm and happy being physically near the ones we love.

Today, instead of a banana or sausage, we use an eggplant emoji to represent something that is rarely (likely never) as large as a full-grown eggplant. An eggplant and three droplets of water can really get the mood going in iMessage. Consequently, vegetarians are more in favor of giving oral sex than non-vegetarians. . . but, that's a conversation for another time.

Provided by OkCupid's extensive data driven platform, I want to share a few facts about sex from today's users of the online dating service.

- A woman has more difficulty achieving orgasm if she does not exercise.
- When men in their 20s described gentle sex, *challenges* was the most used word.
- When women in their 20s described rough sex, *obsessed, piercings,* and *damn* came up most often.
- As men get older, they like sex rougher. A man in his 60s prefers rougher sex than a man in his 20s. #shocker
- The more college tuition someone paid, the more times they would like to have sex in a week. . . Must be the stress.

For those of you that saw "Sex" in the index and immediately jumped to this chapter, I'm not surprised. Sex is one of the most interesting topics. It's raw, vulgar, and sparks everyone's curiosity. If you read this book in order and got to this chapter gradually, I applaud you for making it this far.

I couldn't write about human connection with talking about sex. Sex creates life. It's the rawest and most intimate form of human connection. I would go into detail, but I'm not E.L. James and I'm not writing to fulfill a reader's guilty pleasures.

Traditional dating is changing, and by traditional, I mean misogynist and sexist dating standards set on men and women since the beginning our existence.

Millennials are having less sex than previous generations and we're becoming more conservative with our desires for casual sex. We think it's okay to engage in sex more than previous generations, but it's not what our generation wants, overall. While we're thinking differently about casual sex and more millennials are actually interested in love and relationships, we're also becoming more open to the idea of women being sex-positive. Just because we have more access to finding people who want casual sex due to applications like Tinder, it's a misconception that our generation is only looking for casual pieces and not trying to find deeper connections.

From sexting to snapchat, the digital tease is added as a component of foreplay for many couples.

I'm still not convinced Snapchat was created for any other reason, originally, other than to send provocative photos that will only last temporarily in someone's inbox. Allegedly the idea came about when a fraternity brother of the CEO Evan Spiegel dawned on how he accidently sent a photo to the wrong person. It was something he couldn't undue. Nobody wants their sexy photos to be seen by anyone other than the intended receiver. However, if you know your picture will go away as soon as its seen, that makes a bit easier, right?

As you may know, that's not just the reason Snapchat is used today. The young CEO created a new way of communicating with just photos and videos. It's a way to show your friends real-time, real actions and daily activities, not to show memories. Each day, 170 million people, mostly teens and millennials, send these disappearing messages. Today, Snap Inc. is valued at about $25 billion.

I was using my mom's phone one day and I noticed a notification from Snapchat appeared at the top of her screen. My mom had always said, "Don't get mad if you look through my phone and see something you wish you hadn't." This time, I couldn't resist. I opened the application to see that there was an unopened Snapchat from my dad waiting to be opened. I ignored it and decided to look at my mom's friend list on Snapchat, instead, to see if any of my aunts and uncles were on the application, as well. My dad was her only friend. Immediately, I ran to my mother to question her about her use of the application. "That's none of your business." I didn't even know my parents had a Snapchat, nor realized they knew what it was or how to use it. To this day, neither will admit why they use it and I'll leave that up to the reader's imagination.

While many think the digital era has ruined our intimacy and human connection, social media has actually increased intimacy among people. We are in contact with people almost every minute of every day. We may sometimes feel the need to respond to our partners immediately and feel that we are entitled to a response when we do send a message. Most of our communication is to the same people every single day, furthering and deepening the connections we have with them.

Without exposing too much of my own relationship, I would say having FaceTime is a main reason my long-distance relationship lasted as strong as it did. Watching falling asleep with his face next to mine and hearing the slows of his breath as I drifted off into a deep-sleep as well, were the closest substitute to having him actually next to me. If we were in a long-distance relationship in the early $20^{th}$ century, what would we have done?

While I was abroad, one of my professors' wife was due in a week with their first child. Each afternoon, he would get a call or text from her thinking she was in labor. He apologized each day for having his phone on during class, but we all understood. He couldn't physically be there for her in that moment because he was teaching in Spain, but they lived in Thailand. But, he still wouldn't miss it. His face would light up in hopes that she was having their baby with every ringtone or vibration from his iPhone. He'd immediately tend to her, while still being one of my favorite professors from my time abroad. The love was evident in every swipe to answer.

Intimacy is more than sex. It's feeling the need to step away from your job to talk with your wife or children. It's checking up on someone even when you are occupied with work or family. Intimacy accounts for the 50% or more of people that use their email access at work to send private emails rather than work emails. It's having FaceTime lunches with your boyfriend that lives 4,000 miles away. We are still as intimate as we were without technology but we are now intimate in different ways.

While you can't fully recreate the physical sensations of being with a lover over a phone or tablet, you can recreate an anticipation to the moment. The constant desire for our partners have given emotional and physical intimacy a new meaning in the digital world. Our bodies react to a sexy snapchat the same way we react to a real-life tease. The eggplant emoji will get us excited for the anticipation of what's to come next.

Intimacy isn't just physical, anymore.

## CHAPTER 9

# MANSPACE

*They created these spaces to reflect what they love to do, and who they were.*

—SAM MARTIN, AUTHOR, *MANSPACE: A PRIMAL GUIDE TO MARKING YOUR TERRITORY*

Defined by the Oxford dictionary, the friend zone is a situation in which one member of a friendship wishes to enter into a romantic or sexual relationship, while the other does not. Mario eloquently described the friend zone in his 2002 hit "Just A Friend." He questioned why he couldn't be more than just a friend to the girl he was pursuing. He sang,

*I can be your fantasy, but you say I'm just a friend.*

The story is always the same, no matter the gender or sexual identity. In this case, guy likes girl. Girl dates other guys. Girl tells guy about other guys. Guy gets sad because girl does not like him. Guy does not know what to do.

This platonic relationship has underlying connotations that stem from the social standards of masculinity. Originally coined in the sitcom *Friends,* the friend zone was a result of men not fulfilling their sexual conquests. While it has evolved to not assume that men are just trying to have sex, the friend zone still implies a problematic social structure under the assumption of gender roles. It's perpetuates this idea that the "friendly/nice guy" can't get laid and that men should be able to get laid by whoever they want.

However, the concept of the friend-zone can teach men how to be more emotionally engaged and in tune with their wants and needs. It's a matter of communicating clearly what you want from your partner. However, it's important to note that men have been conditioned to be less emotive, less communicative, and less engaged in relationships.

I analyzed couples on Instagram and observed a pattern. In almost every relationship, heterosexual or homosexual, one partner posts the other more. From the heterosexual relationships I've stalked, the girl will almost always post the guy more.

Does that mean he's cheating? Keeping her a secret?

The answer: Maybe, he just doesn't want to post his partner over and over again.

Men engage differently on social media than women, just as they communicate differently, naturally.

As I dug deeper into what these men were actually posting, especially men that were in a relationship, I noticed a majority of their posts followed a similar trend—either photography, fashion, workouts, suits, or a noteworthy aspect of their physique like beards. Their pages were specifically tailored to their interests. It's not to say guys don't post selfies or boast about their self-image in some way. They are still human and if anything, are more open to sending a direct message to a potential partner than most women. Men use social media similarly to how they use a "manspace."

My grandfather had a manspace, as well as my father. Growing up, I recall my father's manspace being his offices in our homes. It was the only room my mom didn't organize the way she organized every other room in our house.

My grandfather transformed his garage into a place for his artwork, a smoke, or a cup of whiskey. My mother commented on how he would sit in the garage for long periods of time doing who knows what. Recently, my father asked my grandfather, "Why did you always go to the garage? What did you do there?"

*To mind my business,* he responded.

A manspace reinforces the primal nature of a man and the need for a territory. As a man engages with another, they in turn share their space with them. When children come into play, it's another division into their territory. In a more modern context, this space is where any man can escape his partner, young children, and household responsibilities, at least for an hour at a time.

Social media is becoming a digital manspace.

It's a man's way of finding his time, alone, or with his friends, to pay attention to his own interests. The digital manspace is a feed of football, fashion, literature, video games, and anything that a man feels passionate about.

I was shocked to see the amount of detail that went into the physical man-spaces of men who refused to wash their own dishes after they used them. They were neat, defined, and a clear depiction of that man enjoys spending his time doing, whether alone or with his friends.

The digital manspace works as an escape where men can have access to any of their interests online. My brother is constantly on YouTube watching football highlights. My partner is constantly finding Dave Chappelle comedy shows. Statistically, men spend significantly more time on YouTube than women. I don't understand how they could be so tuned in to either of these videos. However, they also wouldn't understand why I can repeatedly watch the same romantic movie. I wouldn't understand why their Instagram feeds don't include as many photos as I would think would be relevant to post and they don't understand why I have a plethora of selfies in my photo album. It's their interests, their spaces, and they have control over them.

CEO of LoveFuckingSucks Brett McGinn is not exactly what you expect from a renowned "relationship expert" on the west coast. He markets himself as being a literal "shoulder to cry on" for women and men who faced heartbreak and broken relationships. I put "relationship expert" in quotes because Brett rarely wants to call himself that. He's just a friend that you can talk to. He offers un-bias relationship advice. He is the male perspective to his female clients and a companion to his male clients, and teaching men the importance of dealing with their own emotions. As a male love consultant, Brett recognized how his own development and gender roles have impacted his relationships, as well as recognized how this pattern impacted his male clients.

The social implications of masculinity impact how men are engaging with their emotions. They are taught to withhold emotion earlier than women. Women learn to withhold emotion as a result of "growing up." Men are taught to withhold emotion at a younger age, as a result of masculinity. It's "emasculating" to be emotive. To prove this is taught, a study from Harvard Medical School analyzed 6-month-old boys in relation to their female counterparts. These infants were more emotive than the female infants. Through age 5, boys tended to cry more and throw tantrums. By age 15, boys tended to show less feelings and affection towards their family and friends. In the field of relationships, boys are less likely to confide in their guy friends and family for emotional support and intimate relationships.* A man's romantic partner will become his primary source of intimacy and support; contrastingly, a woman confides in her romantic partner, friends, and family for those same forms of care. The results in this development are a fear of obtaining support from other males, a lack of emotional stability and a feeling of possessiveness.

Men are indirectly taught that they cannot confide in other men.

The beauty of social media is the comradery that men have also been able to find with other men over shared experiences.

---

* https://www.nytimes.com/2016/04/10/education/edlife/teaching-men-to-be-emotionally-honest.html

As juvenile as it may sound, the #NoShaveNovember movement became source of support for men around the world. In this case, it specifically became a support system for men with prostate cancer. Adam Garone, the founder of Movember (the original #NoShaveNovember), noticed that there was a large community for women coming together to bring awareness about breast cancer. However, in 2004, there wasn't the same global support system for men's health. Comparatively, prostate cancer impacts men at the same rate breast cancer impacts women, in terms of the number of men diagnosed and dying from the sickness. This observation resulted in the #Movember movement. Garone decided to grow a mustache every November to bring awareness to prostate cancer and better engage men with the health risks they face.

He said, "It's about each person coming to this platform, embracing it in their own way, and being significant in their own life." Men became a part of a movement meant to support one another. Ironically, it's a community based on the growth of facial hair. By 2010, Movember generated over 450,000 ambassadors ("Mo Bros" growing mustaches) worldwide, funded prostate cancer foundations in more than 10 countries, and raised over 77 million dollars.

Despite the success of this movement in tackling the lack of support of men's health issues, a sense of male community still lacks on social media. Men are less likely to comment on their male friend's photos. Women are quick to compliment their friends and post obnoxiously excited comments, such as...

*YAAAASSS!*

*I can't even* ■

*OMG! So perf.*

While these comments may seem annoying to men, women are receiving more gratification and self-confidence from their social media accounts than men.

Social media has created niche groups for communities to support one another; however, it will be important for innovators to understand the needs of these groups for human connection. As natural care-takers, women tend to be more caring to other women. As natural competitors, men tend to compete with other men. Men deserve a space to be comforting and caring for one another, just as women are for each other.

Based on our gender, we are raised to think differently. Women have fairytales. Men have adventure quests. Women have Cinderella and Belle. Men have Woody and Buzz Lightyear. From a young age, women are taught to wait for the men. Men are taught to claim the women. These are the narratives we are given in popular media that dictate the behaviors we see in our relationships.

When was the last time you saw a man cry in a movie? It happens, but not as often as women crying on featured films and television shows.

There's a reason men are statistically "angrier" than women. When a child becomes angry, what do they do? They cry, scream, yell, throw objects, hit, kick, and all of the above at the same time. They have a sudden burst of anger and disappointment as a result of that anger. However, these tantrums don't last long. Kids wear their emotions on their sleeves and they're able to get over things quicker. The child will learn to calm down and reassess the situation. It's unlikely that the child will have a tantrum about the exact same situation again because they were already able to release their feelings. Children understand how to deal with their emotions better than adults because they release their emotions in the moment, instead of holding them in. As a result of holding in emotions, adults are more susceptible to depression, anxiety, and other forms of mental illness. This disparity is even greater as it relates to gender.

Second, name a movie where the man's reward in his conquest is NOT a woman. In most adventures, a man's "reward" for fulfilling his quest, winning a war, defeating a villain, etc., is a love interest at the end. Even in Toy's Story, Buddy was rewarded with friendship and Little Bo Peep. Nintendo's Mario fights to save Peach from Bowser's castle. These storylines only evolve as boys get older, but the underlying theme is the same.

A man's emotional vulnerability is only acceptable in private. This is why a man utilizes his private space in any way that he can. He wants to be able to be himself and be his most vulnerable. While social media is a public forum, a man's profile is still his space to share his own sense of individuality. It's the piece of individuality that society tries to define for him. When engaging in romantic relationships, it is imperative that men have a space to feel emotionally vulnerable. However, the relationship cannot be the man's only form of care and support.

All of these behaviors translate into heterosexual relationships. When dating, a majority of men are more likely to withhold emotions, be overtly sexual, and inhibit possessiveness. Because we teach men that women are a prize, love becomes a game. It's a competition for men to see who can win the most hearts or win the best girl. It's a challenge when it comes time to actually express emotions and their needs to the person they are dating.

A note to the fellas reading this:

1. Love isn't a game. It isn't war. It's isn't a reward, nor a conquest. Love is a choice that both men and women have to make.
2. Try flattery. As Brett eloquently stated, "As much as everyone hates being rejected, everyone loves being flattered." No one ever thinks, *Goddamn, can you believe that guy told me I was attractive?*
3. Claim your ManSpace. Be yourself. You deserve a space where you can be emotionally vulnerable, be an individual, and define your own definition of what a man really is.

## CHAPTER 10

# FAIRY TALES

*Fairy tales are more than true: not because they tell us that dragons exist, but because they tell us that dragons can be beaten.*

—NEIL GAIMAN, *CORALINE*, 2004

* *

When I was five, I dressed as Cinderella for Halloween.

When I was eight, I dressed as Snow White.

At the age of ten, I was Belle from Beauty and the Beast.

I watched every movie and hoped to find that love one day. When I was 10, I thought I knew what love was. You couldn't convince me otherwise. Every fairy tale taught me that there will be a happy ending when it comes to love. A guy would approach me one day, or see me at a school dance or a coffee shop in New York and completely fall in love with me in that moment. Now at the age of 21, I learned that love is no fairy tale.

Similar to many young girls, the Disney princesses were the epitome of who I wanted to be. They were beautiful, smart in their own individual ways, and most importantly. . . they found their happily ever after's. These women became princesses by just being who they are and not letting their situations change their values. But, was it their purpose to wait for their prince?

Disney didn't teach us that these ladies had more to do than just wait.

Being Cinderella will not help young girls in the long run. No one tells you exactly how many frogs you have to dig through before you find an eligible gentleman.

To find her prince, and quickly dig through the frogs, Damona Hoffman was an early adopter of online dating. In 2004, she and her husband met via an online dating platform. Not many women her age were using online dating at the time, but that didn't stop Damona. She was ready to find, as she once called it in her blogs, her "Prince Charming."

Unfortunately, dating is never a Disney princess fairy tale.

Consider this scenario:

You stay in your house most of the time, until one evening, you are randomly invited to a party. You dance with your *prince* or *princess* who will not remember exactly who you are. At that moment, you're probably wishing you would've made your move when he/she was actually sober. However, you hope that person wakes up the next morning (likely with a slight hangover) and think "wow, I have to find him/her." To make matters worse, you dropped your college ID and that embarrassing photo from freshman year 4 years ago doesn't quite do you the justice you deserve. Hillary Duff's adaptation of *A Cinderella Story* may have been the closest realistic adaptation of this scenario. But, life just doesn't happen that way, Mr. Disney.

In a society where feminism has become a topic of daily political and social conversation, where we are seeing more women CEO's and political leaders, more global women presidents, paternal leave for fathers so mothers can continue to work, we are beginning see an equal playing field in regards to gender equality. Yet, statistics show that we haven't quite seen these gender roles equalize at the same rate when it comes to dating. Men are undoubtedly still in control because women are told and shown, from a young age, to wait for the Prince to come to you.

However, one CEO is attempting to change the rules of the dating game.

Whitney Wolfe, the founder of Bumble is here to tell you that it is time for you to go after your prince.

I can only recount the types of messages I received from men on Tinder that were very vulgar and uncomfortable. From being cat-called on the street to being cat-called in direct messages, there's no way for women to escape these sexual comments. In no way is this chapter an attack on men, nor is it an assumption on all men. I encourage my male readers to engage in this chapter in order to understand how one woman felt inclined enough to build an application where that cat-call will not occur because women will make the first move. Wolfe created a platform where women are in the driver seat. And, from the experiences of many of my male patrons, they enjoy the feeling of being the one that gets flattered on Bumble, rather than feeling like they have to make the first move. It gives both genders a different feeling from another point on view.

Women feel they need to almost put on a different personality for men.

In many heterosexual relationships, women are the passenger seat drivers without realizing it. By making the first move, you are unexpectedly driving the way the relationship will go because you made that initial push to go for it. Men do this all the time and women find themselves constantly waiting for the next step to come from the man.

We wait for the first message.

We wait for the first date.

We wait for the first kiss.

We wait for the first notion of a committed relationship.

We wait for the guy to decide if moving in together is a good idea.

We wait for the ring.

"The notion of waiting around, or being on the man's terms... I felt it was time to say stop", exclaims Wolfe. "The goal was to give women the control to guide the conversation in the direction they wanted, to take the pressure off the man from maybe thinking he needs to start with something really out there. It allows the women to be like... I'm going to be in the driver's seat."

Studies done by OkCupid show that women are still reluctant to send the first message, no matter age, income level, attractiveness, or any other possible determining factor. Women do not send first messages. To be honest, I rarely send the first message. Because, that's what we are taught to do. Wait. Wolfe's own love story reflected these values as well. She approached him.

They were at a ski resort and she approached him to question his decision to not being skiing since they were at a ski resort. He claimed he didn't know how.

She thought, well, this could be my time to shine and show him my skills so up the gondola they went and to the top of the mountain.

*Go slow so I can keep up*, he claimed.

After helping her click in her skis, a "pro move" according to Wolfe, they went down the mountain. He was just as fast as her and doing all types of tricks.

*He even skied past me going backwards,* she recalled.

When they got to the bottom, he clicked off the skis.

*Y'all have a good day!* He walked off.

Based on that interaction, Wolfe felt in that moment that she found *the one.* They began talking as soon as they both left

Colorado and began dating a month later, on Valentine's Day.

The proposal was just as unexpected as their first encounter, but that's for you all to read on your own. The point is Wolfe practiced what she preached and took lead.

Another successful woman CEO in the dating application industry, Amanda Bradford reiterated that becoming mainstream was not the highlight or the "moment I knew I made it." Social media going mainstream and having a lot of users was not her meter for success. "My biggest moment," Bradford goes on to explain, "was two years ago, the company just turned one, it was the time I realized I was making the most impact. Women of all ages, out of marriages, bad relationships, career-focused, etc. reached out to me after a blog post I put up with the New York Times and told me how my application reminded them to invest in themselves, get out of these unhealthy relationships and build a platform for themselves." She explained how she built a platform that inspired women and that's what mattered.

* *

Amy Webb is a professor, a quantitative futurist, a CEO and an all-around very intelligent woman. She studied game theory, economics, statistics, political science, computer science, sociology, music and journalism. She is one of the top management thinkers to likely shape the future of how organizations are managed. She's a researcher.

In 2012, Amy was another person who experienced a unpredictable ending to a hopeful relationship. She was stuck in the infamous pattern of talk, date, get nowhere but not admit that you're getting nowhere, and end all of a sudden with no clear reason as to why. She was at the end of a bad break up, 30 years old and then planned out this timeline to have reasonable ample time to get into a new relationship, get married and have kids. Name someone who's detailed plan actually worked out the way they planned it.

Living in Philadelphia, she weighed her possible options. While her filters of what she wanted when shopping around weren't too specific, she did want a man who was Jewish and around her age. She also wanted him to not be interested in golf. Without statistical data, I can hypothesize that 75% of men who claim they aren't interested in golf will become interested in golf by at least 50 years old. Depending on Amy's desired age-range for the men she's dating, finding a man not interested in golf might have been to find.

Growing up in a loving family with close siblings, Amy wanted to replicate her own family dynamic. Her loving parents showed what a loving marriage could be like and she remembered all the wonderful memories she had with her siblings. Her siblings were beginning to start their own families and Amy was just not at that point in her life. While she doesn't hint at it, I'm sure there was the awkward, "so when are you having kids, Amy?" questions from Grandma at the family gatherings.

To begin the next chapter of her dating life, Amy took to online dating to find a prospective partner.

Online dating is predicated on an algorithm. Dating sites use data (preferences, type, usage, location, etc.) to match people together and create *inorganic* relationship. What's hilarious about Amy's first profile on social media is that she didn't really have the time nor care to filling it out and genuinely making sure she found real dates. She instead copied her résumé into her dating profile, which, summarized, resembled the following:

> WHAT DO YOU DO: Quantitative Futurist
> WHAT DO YOU LIKE: Studying game theory
> WHAT ARE YOUR INTERESTS: Game theory

To Amy's surprise, the computer matching system gave her what she wanted—guys that matched her job experience, skills and awards.

Her first date was with an IT guy—they shared a love for gadgets and data. She detailed that the date didn't go well. They were incompatible. A series of similar dates occurred and Amy realized that although she was getting matched with men that shared her résumé, they just weren't going to be her Prince Charming. It's a difficult situation because, as she details in her story, "These probably weren't bad guys. They were just bad for me. The algorithms that were setting us up weren't bad either. These algorithms were doing exactly what they were designed to do . . . The real problem here is that the algorithms work just fine, you and I don't."

So, what did Amy do? She decided to forge her love of data and JavaScript with her desire to find love. She decided to "reverse-engineer" the algorithm by kind of making it work to her benefit.

Firstly, she created a long list of her desires:

- Jewish
- Family-oriented
- Hard worker
- Smart
- Loved adventure and travel

And many, many, many more. After organizing this data, she then created a scoring system to see what would be her way of calculating how much she likes the men she finds based on her desires. Specifically, if someone reached 700 points, they could receive an email, 900 points could receive a date, and 1500 points could have the potential to be a long-term relationship. Her efforts were astonishing. It made me wonder if I did enough work when finding my partner.

Second, while Amy could like her Prince Charming, she needed her Prince Charming to like her. She then researched the type of women that would like the same men she liked. I won't go into detail of how she did this, but she learned how to maximize her profile and learned what it took for men to want to message her and engage with her online. Four things mattered most:

- **Content**—How much information is on your profile (Less is more!)
- **Optimistic language**—Easy, positive, happy words
- **Timing**—The best times that has the highest user engagement
- **Photos**—First impressions matter, right? Be yourself, but an attractive version of yourself

After recreating her profile and tricking the algorithm to giving her what she wants, she then just needed to score these men and see if they were 700 points worth her time. Most weren't but one special Prince Charming was.

Today, Amy is a married woman, with a daughter named Petra. She is the woman who utilized her core competencies to get what she wants. She didn't change who she was nor did she settle for anything less than what she wanted and deserved. Anyone who believes they can't find love without changing who they are and what they believe in will learn from Amy's story. Amy is adamant about the power of data and utilized her talents to find herself a Prince Charming. Her happily ever after came from her being true to her interests, her "pickiness" and her core.

* *

In my own relationship, without even realizing it, I made those first moves. My current partner and I recounted our initial moments differently and I loved the way he told the story because he gave me most of the credit for beginning this relationship.

We met via the application, GroupMe, a group messaging application for generally large groups and people with iPhones to escape the annoying green messages on iMessage. I was looking for housing for a summer internship and it was normal for young adults to message in these group chats for instances like this. In the specific group chat I messaged, I was able to contact with students from University of Miami.

He replied stating that there was a sublet in the 6 bedroom co-ed home where he resided.

After initially messaging each other on GroupMe, I asked him for his number. It's easier than constantly checking GroupMe and I needed his number anyway since he was going to become my housemate.

Our first physical meeting was an interesting moment in that I felt instantly curious about him. And he later admitted he felt the same way. When I recount the first interactions of me being in the house, I remember just being friendly because I had no one else to converse with or talk to. I was in intern in a new city and I really didn't know anyone. When he recounts the story, I was constantly trying to talk to him and genuinely get to know him. I would sit down with him and begin random conversations. Those random and interesting conversations over time sparked a connection.

After a couple of weeks of settling in the house and interning, he invited me out to a house party with a couple of his Greek brothers. I was excited to meet other members of my sorority as well, but I was also excited to go with him. The car ride was 45 minutes and it was the perfect time for us to continue talking and getting to know each other outside of living in the same space.

He recounts that I asked so many questions about his past, but he admits he was happy I did. We talked about relationships in general, and little did I know, although I wasn't physically in the driver's seat, but I drove that conversation.

When we got to the party, our body language immediately shifted. Everyone in that party thought we were together from the way we interacted with each other. He would offer to get me anything I needed, we would make eye contact from across the room at the party. We were constantly caught whispering and laughing about who knows what. Throughout the evening, he would check on me and make sure I was enjoying myself.

From that moment, we were inseparable during the rest of the summer. One day when we were recounting the events from that evening, he alleged,

"You know you kissed me first that night, right?"

I was shocked! I do not remember that happening in the way he recounted, or I was choosing not to remember. I denied it every time he said I kissed him first. . . but then I realized, why should that be something I'm not proud of?

When we were on our way back home from the party, we had to stop at the gas station. I remember being in and out of sleep because it was so late and I was tired. I woke up for a slight second. He came over to my window after beginning to pump the gas. From my recount, I rolled down my window and we were caught in that movie-scene moment where we locked eyes, he leaned in over the window, I leaned back towards him, and at that point a kiss was inevitable.

His recount (and likely the accurate one):

> *I came over to your window to see if you wanted anything from inside. I knocked on the window so that you would roll it down. You rolled it down. I leaned in, asked if you wanted a snack from the gas station, and then . . . you kissed me. You just went for it with no hesitation. Hashtag. I. Was. Not. Ready.*

It's 2018.

Bumble was created for moments like this. After years without realizing it, I was allowing men to define the terms by expecting my prince charming to come along and sweep me off my feet. Who knew I just needed to swipe on GroupMe to direct message someone? Or, roll down my window and initiate a first kiss? My 10-year-old hopeless romantic self would have never approved.

Many women dating experts encourage female clients to send the first message, no matter what social media or dating platform you utilize, because men send first messages at a rate 3x more than women. Research has also shown that women are more likely to get a response from the guys they truly want if the send the first message. When you send the first message, you're bringing attention to your profile. You surpass the competition and going after what you truly want. Men do this all the time. Women who continue to wait for the first message are settling without even realizing it. Women are 2.5x more likely to get a response than men if they initiate. If you're a woman who sends the first message, not only are you more likely to get more responses in general, but you'll be having conversations with more attractive guys. If you are single and looking for a relationship, you have nothing to lose when sending a message, first. Bumble is reminding millennials and post-millennials that times are changing and we all should be going for what we want if we want a relationship. When you are dating, you deserve to choose who you want and feel confident in that decision.

So, ladies, let's stop being Cinderella.

# CHAPTER 11

# COMPATIBILITY

*The propensity to make strong emotional bonds to particular individuals is a basic component of human nature.*

—JOHN BOWLBY, AUTHOR, *A SECURE BASE: PARENT-CHILD ATTACHMENT AND HEALTHY HUMAN DEVELOPMENT*

Dr. Chapman says you should just ask yourself one question about your partner:

*What do they complain about the most?*

He's known as many things. The Christian love guru. The marriage savior. The pastor.

When Dr. Gary Chapman began working in the local church, he realized the main struggle in people's lives was their marriage. He claims he was thrown into this business.

*I had the personality that listens and empathizes*

When beginning to work in the field, he realized like many others that you just need two things to become a credible dating or marriage counselor—the ability to listen to other people's problems and some type of dating experience.

He has now been married for over 50 years.

Now, I'm sure some of you are asking yourselves "Devin, what can an 80-year old Southern Baptist pastor can tell me about Tinder or why my DMs aren't popping?" Well, he probably can't tell you much of anything regarding specific social media practices. But his skills and knowledge of love languages teach us to look past the digital sphere of what we know as dating now and return to our natural human instinct. While marriage may seem out of reach for the average millennial and post-millennial, Dr. Chapman's languages apply not only to the long-lasting commitment, but will also teach us how we can get the most out of our day-to-day dating lives and our platonic relationships.

Dr. Chapman collected notes from all his clients. When he re-read them, line by line, he noticed a clear pattern in the details people would tell him about the problems in their marriages:

*I feel like they don't love me anymore.*

*I don't understand why. Look at all the things I do for you.*

*You don't spend enough time with me.*

*You never do anything for me.*

After reading twelve years of notes from counseling, he realized each issue fell into one of five categories- quality time, words of affirmation, receiving gifts, acts of service, and physical touch.

When you learn how to speak the other person's love language, you better understand what it takes for that person to feel loved or fulfilled in the relationship. We're all different and we feel love in different ways. While you may feel love by receiving gifts from your partner, your partner may not feel love in that same way.

Dr. Chapman recalls, *My wife's love language is acts of service. I take the trash out and the woman is happy.*

A significant tip that Dr. Roz gave me is to be **observant.** Similar to what Dr. Chapman says, it's important to understand who your partner is, what they want and what makes them feel loved. For some reason, I immediately thought of the importance of each step in this process. Whether it's evaluating a potential partner in real life or digitally, the process still looks the same. It's in our nature to want to be compatible with another being.

*He lost his job when the economy took a hit in 2008-2009. It was rough in the relationship. However, being observant and knowing him, I was comfortable in knowing that he was a hard worker and I was honestly not worried about him finding a job eventually. When he lost his job, I didn't want to freak out.*

*Back when we were just dating, he picked up a part-time job to help me out because I was in school and couldn't work full-time. So, I knew he had this character trait of taking care of me and being a provider and being a protector.*

*When he lost his job, it wasn't a panic. It was a 'We'll get through this. What do I have to do? How can I help you?' I did email blasts to any and every company I knew people at, didn't know anyone at, any company I could find. It became a real partner step and strengthened our relationship.*

*Because I had gone through that season with him, of really observing him and knowing that when times get rough, he will take care of me and he is a caretaker, it was easy for me to say yes when he proposed. And, today, he was a well-paying job and we are okay.*

I had the privilege of asking Dr. Roz to share when she knew it was love. She detailed that from the very beginning she knew he was the one because of how open, genuine and secure he was with her. He assured her, "you can talk to me about anything." He provided her with emotional security and that was something she was not used to having prior to this relationship.

After recognizing your attraction to someone, what do you feel you can gain from a prospective date? Is there a possibility for the relationship to become more than just friends? What is the probability of a second date?

Are you two compatible?

I'm not asking you all to create an excel spreadsheet or detail a list like Amy Webb, but it is important to do your research and trust your gut. Instilled in us is a conscience that will usually offer a clear first impression of your compatibility with another person or passion. When researching, while you cannot be 100% sure of your hypothesis without conducting the experiment, you should be able to construct a *smart* hypothesis worth testing.

These observations are over a period of time. It's not simply a day or a week. **You must go through seasons with someone.**

I don't mean the physical seasons. You must go through periods of happiness, periods of stress, periods of sadness, and all the other *seasons* that we experience. The *seasons* are key to analyzing how two can become one unit in the relationship. Engaging romantically with another cannot be forced because of the psychological and biological factors that tie into these emotional connections. Analyzing simply how someone makes you their #MCM and #WCW each week will not give you the deep results you need in this experiment to make a sound conclusion.

I remember when I was asked about my own relationship. I felt early on that my partner and I could have a long-term relationship. "What do you love about him?" When asked this question, I rarely responded with adjectives, but rather stories and instances that made me fall in love with him. From our very first interaction, he was a gentleman. He constantly offered and then proceeded to help me with any task. When I would think these acts were solely to impress me, I noticed how he would hold the door open for families and the elderly when we were in public spaces. He would give up his seat—his own comfort—for the comfort of others. He consistently checked in on his friends and family to ensure they were okay. When leaving the grocery store, he would offer to carry people's bags if they needed. I remember when I was laying with him one day, and he told me to leave the room while he called his mother in order to give his mother the appropriate private time for their relationship. This was a man I knew would always be a gentleman.

He always opened the door for me, allowed me to be seated before he is, checked on me throughout my day, respected our private conversations, and offered and then proceeded to give me any help I may need. I observed these actions and expected nothing less from him.

What makes each day worth taking these risks are the rewards. Ask yourself: What's compatible with you? What makes you feel loved? What simply makes you happy?

People are taking more risks to find these answers because of social media. We have access beyond our physical scope and that's something we haven't had before.

I cut all my hair off in high-school because of Instagram. I saw several beautiful women on a daily basis with short-hair flourishing. Seems very adolescent, but have you never been inspired by something you saw on social media? For hours, I'd look at "pixie cut" styles and each day I would convince myself I'm ready to do it, until it was 11:59 PM and then I suddenly wasn't. Then one day, I just did it. It was fun . . . and short-lived. But, if the platform, in this case, Instagram, had not been available, I never would have cut my hair. Through social media, I was able to connect, virtually, with random women who inspired me with their style and grace. If I had not seen a representation of women I felt connected to, my hair wouldn't have been cut. At the time, doing something like that felt very risky and exciting for me because it wasn't anything I was used to doing.

Sometimes, we risk throwing away our financial stability to follow our passions. New York is known for many things, including the 9 to 5 (which really means 6:30 to 8) white collar workers convincing themselves that investment banking is their passion. They turn to many different tools that keep them sane, especially when their job just isn't cutting it. These social platforms are the sources of creativity and comfort.

Dale Choonoolal, for instance, was one of these investment bankers in New York. He began to set up Meetup's for people in the city who loved soccer and set up pick-up soccer games. After the popularity of his meetups grew, he was able to turn them into income. What began in 2008 as a way to meet other soccer loves in the urban jungle is now NYCSoccer.com, a six-figure business that began from following a passion for soccer. Now, most of Choonoolal's time is setting up the co-ed soccer league. To date, he has connected 12,221 soccer lovers.

We risk falling in love with someone that may be 10,000 miles away because, why not? When you can FaceTime, texts, and build on your friendship solely based on conversation, and the relationships are still genuine and organic, why not, I ask. Distance makes the heart grow fonder, *they* say.

*He'll forget all about it, because this is from Tinder. This is just what tends to happen.*

One of my girlfriends utilized Tinder while she was abroad, as well. As soon as she was ready to stop swiping while away in Japan, she told herself five more minutes, but had her doubts. As if it was fate, she found a guy that was what we all know is her type—tall and well-dressed. Seriously, the first thing she looks at on a guy is his shoes. She skimmed his Instagram. From his neat dreadlocks to the Kanye-like jackets over camo pants and Nikes, and the casual lit flick next to a train rail, she loved his style. He was cute in the face, too.

Their first plans were a shopping trip. Their style is how they bonded . . . and their social connections.

That night, she was wearing MCM jeans with her black patent boots, sheer blouse complimented by a black bralette underneath. A seemingly casual look with a pinch of sexy was her usual. None of her looks would be completed without the gold accents in her ears, around her neck and on her wrist.

*This is an area with at least 100 hundred people crossing the street daily. I was waiting for my friends and I look up from sending the 'Where you at' text and I saw him.*

The bright yellow shirt may have been what helped him stand out. Or, maybe it was because he was super tall. The orange glasses she noticed from 100 feet away also complimented his entire aura. Eyeing him down to the grey pants and the clean white Nikes, she knew it was the guy she swiped right on a few nights ago and had been texting all day. This wasn't the night they planned to meet but she approached him, anyway.

*I initiated the flirting.* This was also, very much, her personality and her style.

He had three more days in Japan before he had to return to Germany. They spent nearly every moment together until he left. From comparing Germany to the U.S., talking about music and style to taking the casual Instagram flick showing off their gold grills in their mouths, each day was cherished because they did not know what to expect once they both left Japan and resided on opposite sides of the Atlantic Ocean. His FILA complimented her Zara. His Palace never overshadowed her BAPE. His retro always welcomed her class with respect and care that she adored to this day.

*He missed his flight. We were together for one more day.*

It wasn't long before our friend group was hearing all about him and how he may have been her soul mate. It worked for months and realistically, they were both not ready for a relationship. It's not because he's in Germany and she's here in the U.S. However, they're still great friends to this day. They still Facetime weekly and text even more so.

*Come to Germany,* he said.

* *

What may be trivial for one person may be meaningful for another. What's beautiful is that as individuals, we are able to define what is meaningful to us.

Sometimes the just because is opening up Snapchat and seeing that your significant other posted you telling his followers that he misses you. It's your grandma writing an embarrassing post on Facebook that is filled with typos but you get the point she was trying to say. Just because's are flowers waiting for you at your house on Valentine's Day. Or, going to a soccer meetup to meet new people that hate their job as much as you do.

This is what compatibility with your internal impulses and your external relationships look like. Finding compatibility with yourself means finding your passions and what makes you an individual and in turn, being compatible with another being. When your day-to-day life is not fulfilling, find the things that are in harmony with who you are.

CHAPTER 12

# DIGITAL TATTOOS

*Do you want to be a trend, or do you want to last forever?*

—SHAWN 'JAY-Z' CARTER

In 2017, 38% of the generation that "can't seem to commit to anything" committed to a permanent mark on their body before turning 30. It was reported that 38% of young people between the ages of 18 and 29 have at least one tattoo. Every tattoo has a story. Even if it's "I got it because I wanted to," it's a representation of an individual's personal choice that they couldn't have made for anyone but themselves.

*It says 'A queen will always turn pain into power.'*

One of my closest sisters told me the story of one of my favorite of her tattoos. She always said that she would get a tattoo when something significant in her life occurred, usually something not so good, like when she got into an argument with mother or her former partner from an unhealthy relationship. It was her way of coping and dealing with her own pain. Interestingly enough, she got her first tattoo as a freshman in college. Every semester after that, a new symbol was drawn onto her body just as every semester she began to grow into her own individuality. Each moment and conquest of hers is shown by the tattoos on her body.

*They're sequential.*

As women, it's easy to feel like our bodies are not really ours. Society tells us what we should do with our bodies, whether it's political or a social stigma. As someone who believes in the Christian word of God, she always thought it was ironic that she truly believed her body was temple not meant to be desecrated.

*However, my tattoos are my control over what all the forces around me tell me I shouldn't control, as a woman. My body is a temple. It's my temple and I'm doing what I want to it. I'm making it my own. I'm reclaiming it.*

She reminded me that beyond our bodies, the events in our lives are completely out of our control. Each tattoo tells her story of an uncontrollable event in her life that has impacted her entire being and continues to shape her to the women she is. It was the uncontrollable factors that led her to a choice that she has full control over.

This tattoo specifically was the one she hesitated the most on. The word *queen* meant more to her than she originally thought it meant to her. A *queen* is the utmost highest ranked woman, royalty, beauty, and power. Her hesitation stemmed from feeling like she could not live up to that word. She questioned, "am I actually a queen?"

With everything she's been through, she was always told by her own mother and lovers that she was not a queen. She was not worthy.

*As soon as I posted my tattoo on social media, my former partner quickly began to degrade me. He began to degrade my use of the word and only reinforced my hesitation that I was not worthy. Putting this tattoo on my body was one of the most nervous I had been getting something on my body. Getting it, I felt strong. Afterwards, I felt I had out-defined myself.*

*Yet, I came to realize... The pain he caused me, I indeed turned it into my own power by overcoming every comment, jab, insult he made about me. And, I asserted this myself. It was my assertion of my queenliness, my sense of self, my faith in myself that I am worthier of being a queen, as all women should feel they are.*

Her tattoo defined her, by her own definition. It was her way of asserting who she felt she authentically was and who she was going to continue to grow to be. The power of a permanent mark on your body is that it is permanent (for the most part) and is an authentic choice made by the individual. Each tattoo on her body was a representation of her. Furthermore, it was a representation of her own decisions.

*I'm no longer in a place where I need a coping mechanism to deal with my pain. I'm healthier now.*

The conversation concluded with the self-reflection of her own growth. She feels comfortable with her past and while tattoos were her response to the *bullshit* that occurred in her life, she now knows how to deal with those moments in healthier ways and is moving past them.

*I don't think I want anymore tattoos.*

* *

I asked in the Chapter 1, Are you truly your authentic self on social media? Are you honest with your individuality? It's very easy for people on social platforms to show a misconception of who they really are. Who they are, who they want to be, and who they are expected tend to become misconstrued and blurred in their own eyes. It's very common nowadays for social media influencers to go offline for a while after realizing the contrast between who they are and their followers' perception of who they are. The emotional stress this can cause on an individual is unhealthy for their own personal emotional intelligence, mental health and impede on one's relationship with their social platform.

Authenticity is feeling comfortable with who you are and comfortable being different from those around you. Both individuals and corporations must deal with figuring out their authentic identity in their lifetime.

Jerry McLaughlin, co-founder and CEO of Branders.com, defines brand as "the perception someone holds in their head about you, a product, a service, an organization, a cause, or an idea."

When I was in seventh grade, my teacher asked each student to take out a piece of paper and write down certain characteristics about ourselves. I wish I could tell you what I wrote back then. I'm pretty sure every year that image would have changed because every year we evolve to who we want to be. What my teacher didn't tell us is that it didn't matter what we thought our brand was because McLaughlin said it best in that a brand is based on a perception *someone else's mind.*

What you put out is what you'll receive in this world. This logic goes for businesses, as well. If you put out lower priced products, expect to receive consumers who are price-conscious. If you put out higher-quality, more expensive products, expect to receive consumers who are quality driven and/or luxurious.

The red and white Coca-Cola logo is recognized by 94% of the world's population. That's approximately 7.1 billion people. In Mandarin, Coca-Cola means "Delicious Happiness." It makes me wonder what came first, the translation or the brand. Coca-Cola prides itself in being many things, and one of those things is not being Pepsico. The brands are different.

They were the original red vs. blue gang competition. If you are not familiar with the Cola Wars, then you probably live in a community where one company completely dominates the market, like Atlanta, where Coca-Cola is headquartered. This war has lasted for now more than 120 years. For a while, the relationship between the two wasn't a war at all, but rather a little brother (Pepsico) trying to keep up with their big brother (Coca-Cola), but never quite making it. The two constantly evolved its products to become better than the other. However, Coca-Cola gracefully kept its success in the beginning by not worrying about Pepsi at all and continuously investing in itself to improve its own brand identity. After merging with Frito-Lay in the mid-60s, Pepsico finally saw success over

Coca-Cola as finally, our favorite couch-potato snacks finally came together under one company.

Coke did not realize it's brand power when things got a bit too personal. The famous "Pepsi Challenge" where little brother challenged big brother in a blind taste test. The unfortunate results for Coke showed that Pepsi was the preference solely based on taste. Years later, the infamous "New Coke" was an utter failure. Coke got a little too sensitive about the taste challenge and decided to change what decades of Coke lovers loved. They changed who they were to appease their competition.

Everyone hated it, 87% of Coke-drinkers to be exact. Protests were enacted. Pepsi laughed as it finally was able to get a shot at its older brother. A little over two months after New Coke launched, *Classic* Coke came back.

Simon Sinek says, "People don't buy what you do; they buy why you do it. And what you do simply proves what you believe." In other words, people don't invest in what you offer. They invest in what you believe. They want to see who you are as an individual. Social media platforms give us the power to show who we are at our own disposal.

"What happens if Facebook, Google, Twitter, LinkedIn, cell phones, GPS, Foursquare, Yelp, Travel Advisor, all these things you deal with every day turn out to be electronic tattoos? And what if they provide as much information about who and what you are as any tattoo ever would?" asked Juan Enriquez, Futurist/TedTalk-er.

Most of every digital piece of information we put out into the world is permanent. Even when something is deleted, the databases of these social media platforms have hold of the information and photos we posted. Some things we choose not to delete. I have a friend that has 2,412 posts on Instagram. As someone who has deleted and recreated their Instagram three times, I could not imagine having that many; however, it makes sense for someone who has been on the platform for almost 6 years.

Every time I deleted my Instagram, I remember feeling like I wasn't who I was posting. It was not necessarily because I was trying to be someone else, but I was constantly changing who I wanted to be. I was constantly evolving and changing at a rapid pace, as someone between the ages of 10-12 should be.

In this new digital era, we have access to everyone's information from the past and present. My friend has six years' worth of memories on her Instagram. Any of us can dig on our pages and figure out key moments in our lives we are proud of and maybe a few that we are not so proud of.

**We're all stalkers.**

When you look at one friend's Twitter, you may see that she values music, finding new artists, promoting new songs, engaging in conversations about extended playlists (EPs), and lyrics.

When you look at another friend's Twitter, his tweets may show how he cares about the way he's treated in relationships. He tweets about valuing clear communication and not giving second chances. His transparency gives anyone interested in him, his expectations and history in relationships in 140 characters or less.

When you look at my twitter, I'm the hopeless romantic. Most of my tweets are the #RelationshipGoals, lyrics from love songs, reposting other people's relationships and love stories. That's who I am and what I'm interested in.

One of the great aspects of technology is that we are able to expedite the research process of someone we may be interested in engaging with. On a broader scale, you can find out if the person is even available for a dating relationship. When you connect with someone on social media, you get the opportunity to get a glimpse of their life by previewing their pages. We can use social media to gain an idea of who the person might be, who they like, what they dislike, what types of content they post on Instagram, their photos on Facebook, how they spend quality time, their interests. People will tend put out what they feel is most important and valuable to them.

However, it's also important to be careful because of how permanent your choices may be. I'm sure we can think of one person, familiar or not, that has regretted a tattoo on their body. While it was the past, the past may be able to come to the light due to the technology at every individual's fingertips. Pepsico, to this day, is still apologizing for the Kendall Jenner ad that reimagined protests against police brutality. Dove is constantly apologizing for the racist advertisement that showed a black woman becoming a white woman after using Dove soap. Yes, this is an old mistake that Dove made, however, Black Twitter will never let Dove live that one down.

Our digital decisions are just as important and permanent as our real ones. And, with the growing access we have to everyone around us, we must also know what are we branding about ourselves? Who are you telling people you are and is that the accurate perception of who you are?

Instagram reminds us that while these highlighted moments on our feeds are important to us, people are much more than that. What you see is not always what you are getting and it's those moments when you can be your most authentic that determine the extent to which what people are seeing is exactly what they are getting.

When people are looking at your profiles, what are they seeing? Are you giving off the impression that you want to give? Are you being you or are you Coke trying to be Pepsi? This is the value of authenticity.

A liked page on someone's Facebook can tell you about their interests. A post on Instagram can tell you about their experiences. A tweet on Twitter can tell you how a person thinks. These are our tattoos. Every tattoo represents something that I've experienced. Everything you see on me, I can tell you what happened. Each word we've ever tweeted, every photo on Instagram, every like on Facebook is our permanent mark in the digital world.

## CONCLUSION

# THE POWER OF HELLO

*What's the secret to long-lasting relationships?*
*Not breaking up.*

—UNKNOWN

It was the fall of '84 that changed my life, forever.

Brian was the new guy in high-school. A transferring senior. Tall. Curly dark hair. Large almond eyes. The girls already couldn't resist his charm and the smile he gave after telling one of his corny jokes was his signature. That was topped off with the one crooked left tooth he had, but some people found it cute. For a while, Brian was occupied with the squad of girls he had as his fans, but there was one young lady that changed the chemistry of the room on the rare occasions that he happened upon her. She was petite, brown-skinned, mid-length thick black beautiful hair, and always had a large back-pack that she carried around. She was beautiful, kind of quiet and always walked with purpose from what he had seen of her, which wasn't much at the time.

He would ask his friends about her but without a name, he found it pretty hard to find her in the large multi-floor public school in New York. I mean, how many petite Black girls with black hair are out there, right? Well, eventually, through a friend's friend's sister, he figured out her first name. With a name, he spent a couple of weeks inquiring about her. Did she have a boyfriend? What was she like? Who were her friends? What did she like to do for fun? . . . Did she have a boyfriend? No one knew anything except that everyone knew her father who was a well-respected business owner in the community. She lived on the "right" side of town.

While loitering in the hallways with his bestfriend, Pat, Brian caught a glimpse of her while at a friend's locker. Her locker happened to be around the corner.

*I remember watching her at her locker. I never felt nervous to talk to girls, but Debbie was different.*

She was beautiful, quiet, but also kind of mean, mostly when she didn't want to be bothered. She was wearing red jeans, that day. Her hair was nicely done, always out and styled. Five minutes have gone by and yes, Brian was still peeking from around the corner.

*Brian, when are you going to just talk her, man?*

Pat gave him a bit of courage to finally remember he had game and he needed to go talk to her sooner rather than later. That bit of courage worked—courage being Pat literally nudging him into her direction.

*I almost knocked her 5'1" petite body over.*

She was looking at him kind of crazy and very much giving off the impression that she's not amused, nor impressed, nor going to him any piece of mind.

*Hey.*

She barely looked at him, almost acting like he wasn't standing right by her side trying to get attention. Instead, her line of sight was focused on sending her friends facial signals to inquire about what she should do about this guy. Eyebrows raised translated to, "What do you all think?" After a few words and chuckles from her friends...

*Can I walk you to class?*

She said "if you feel like you need to", but the eternal optimist in him took that as a strong YES.

*Would you like for me to carry your backpack?*

With an untrusting look, she cautiously said

*Sure.*

The weight of the bag caught him off guard... *What the hell do you have in here?*

*'Books! We're in school! Where are yours?'*

The conversation continued as he asked... *Do you have a boyfriend?*

*'Yes, you want to see his picture?'*

Un-phased, he surprised her with... *Yeah, sure.*

She opens her wallet and shows him a young man with a full beard who was the captain of his football team at another high school.

*How old is he?*

He was 16 years old. The exchange continued as he walked her to her advanced math class, getting her there late, which would be the first of many occasions over the years.

*You know, she gave me her number that day. I still have the piece of ripped paper she wrote her number on to this day.*

Thirty-three years later, they had four kids together. I am their youngest.

* *

My book began as research detailing how social media had impacted dating and romantic relationships. I wanted to tell stories of love and stories of break up and hopeless romantic things that relate to the new generations—the sweet sound of a good morning text or a surprise #WCW post or a disappointing "he's tweeting but not texting me back" story. As I continued to read, listen, write and learn more and more about the interconnection between technology and relationships, I realized that these are not just dating stories. These are not just experts that help people find love. The tools we have at our disposal today are not for finding love, going on dates and hoping to find someone to marry.

They are about human connection, and in some way, every connection you have started with a form of hello. In today's digital era, a new hello has emerged and it's called the swipe.

Every hello is a beginning of a new experience, whether that experience lasts a lifetime or a moment. Each hello has a slight effect on us in every way and may lead to our most impactful and significant moments of our lives.

Without that hello from my dad to my mom, and thanks to Uncle Pat for the extra push, I wouldn't be here today. If there's one thing my parents instilled in me, it was to love and be loved. Despite their challenges, they love no matter what. And most importantly, I learned not to only love those I'm familiar with but love people and humanity around me and love life.

Brené Brown, researcher and storyteller, said it best when she said her in TedTalk in 2010 that **vulnerability is the root of connection.**

Being vulnerable is one of the scariest feelings we face because as territorial creatures, we're stubborn. We don't want to feel weak, ever. Unfortunately, we don't correlate weakness as just the absence of strength. Weakness is discomfort. It's leaving a job for your passions. Weakness is telling someone you love them first. However, none of those are weaknesses at all.

Being vulnerable is being your truest self. It's allowing yourself to be authentic and not knowing the consequences. Isn't that what life is about? Not knowing what's going to happen and living it to your fullest anyway? It's a rewarding feeling when you receive the outcome you hoped for, and it's even more rewarding when you put a genuine effort in representing your truest self. A *hello*, so simple yet so vital to our human existence, is the backbone of human connection. When you say hello, you open yourself up to the unexpected and to being vulnerable. You become open to an unexpected conclusion. You connect when you're allowing yourself to be who you are, unapologetically.

You open yourself up to fear in the same moment you open yourself up to strength. Many women who were inspired by Amanda Bradford's story and her dating application reopened themselves up to the possibility of finding a relationship. For some of those women, they overcame fear by finding the strength to re-engage with love with less focus on their career.

You open yourself up to goodbye in the same moment you open yourself up to hello. When the guy that watched the girl talk about her virginity on YouTube took the time to engage with her via social media, and eventually in real life, they knew what they were getting themselves into by being in a long-distance relationship. They were willing to engage in their new relationship that moment they saw each other in person, despite the possibility that their goodbye could have been the last time they connected.

You open yourself to hate in the same moment you open yourself up to love. So, why be afraid to risk the opportunity for failure when you're risking the opportunity for a lasting connection?

The digital era has advanced our tools for human connection. We can connect beyond the scope of our physical boundaries because the digital boundaries are just the areas without an LTE or WiFi signal. Online dating and social networking has created a new wave of allowing ourselves to be vulnerable by giving us the opportunity to show who we are authentically.

Each swipe, double-tap, like, favorite, DM, snap, tweet, and hashtag is a new tool for connection and a new variation of hello.

So, just keep swiping.

# ACKNOWLEDGMENTS

First and foremost, I would like to thank my parents for teaching me what love is, how to love, and how to be patient with love. I'm blessed to have grown up being able to see what love looks like.

I especially want to thank my friends that were vulnerable with me and allowed me to share their experiences and stories in this book. We all have significant experiences that shape each and every one of us and being able to share you all's diverse stories and experiences made this book all the better.

Thank you to the support of Georgetown faculty and staff—Patricia Grant, Jennifer Wiggins, and Daviree Velazquez Phillip. Each of you shaped me into the person that was able to complete this project.

A special thanks to the people that took the time to speak with me, on multiple occasions. It's been such a gratifying experience to learn from each of you. Not only did I learn from your careers and expertise, each of you shared your lives with me. And, I thank you for that.

Finally, a very special thank you to Eric Koester, Brian Bies, and the New Degree Press publishers, editors, and everyone involved in this process. *They* say there are three things everyone should do in their lifetime; one of them is *write a book*. Continue to push to give young authors the opportunity to fulfill this mantra. The opportunity is an amazing gift for which I will be forever grateful.

Thank you everyone for your support throughout this process. From checking in with me constantly to pushing me to believe I could actually write this, and overall, being excited for this project, each of you gave me the push and confidence I needed to finish this. You all were excited about this book before I even knew what it would be about, and somehow, each of you knew that I would choose to write about love and relationships.

# REFERENCES

Atanasova, Aleksandra. “Gender-Specific Behaviors on Social Media and What They Mean for Online Communications.” *Social Media Today*, 6 Nov. 2016, www.socialmediatoday.com/social-networks/gender-specific-behaviors-social-media-and-what-they-mean-online-communications.

Baquet, Dean. Jay-Z. “On therapy, politics, marriage, the state of rap and being a black man in Trump's America.” *The New York Times*.

Bhasin, Kim. “Coke Vs. Pepsi: The Amazing Story Behind The Cola Wars.” *Business Insider*, Business Insider, 2 Nov. 2011, www.businessinsider.com/soda-wars-coca-cola-pepsi-history-infographic-2011-11.

Bialik, Kristen, and Katerina Eva Matsa. “Key Trends in Social and Digital News Media.” *Pew Research Center*, 4 Oct. 2017, www.pewresearch.org/fact-tank/2017/10/04/

key-trends-in-social-and-digital-news-media/.

Bowlby, John. *A Secure Base: Parent-Child Attachment and Healthy Human Development*. Basic Books.

Bradford, Amanda. *The League*, launched Jan. 2015, www.theleague.com/.

Bradford, Amanda. "I'm Not An Elitist, I'm Just An Alpha Female." *LinkedIn*, 20 Oct. 2015, www.linkedin.com/pulse/im-elitist-just-alpha-female-amanda-bradford/.

Brown, Brené. "The Power of Vulnerability." *TED: Ideas Worth Spreading*, TEDxHouston, June 2010, www.ted.com/talks/brene_brown_on_vulnerability.

Chapman, Gary D. *The 5 Love Languages*. Northfield Pub., 2015.

Clifford, Catherine. "How a Tinder Founder Came up with Swiping and Changed Dating Forever." *CNBC*, CNBC, 6 Jan. 2017, www.cnbc.com/2017/01/06/how-a-tinder-founder-came-up-with-swiping-and-changed-dating-forever.html.

Crook, Jordan. "Burned." *TechCrunch*, TechCrunch, 9 July 2014, techcrunch.com/2014/07/09/whitney-wolfe-vs-tinder/.

Dorsey, Jack. Twitter, founded Mar. 2006, www.twitter.com/.

Enriquez, Juan. "Your Online Life, Permanent as a Tattoo." *TED: Ideas Worth Spreading*, TED2013, Feb. 2013, www.ted.com/talks/juan_enriquez_how_to_think_about_digital_tattoos.

Fincher, David, director. *The Social Network*. Sony Pictures Home Entertainment, 2011.

Galloway, Scott. "How Amazon, Apple, Facebook and Google Manipulate Our Emotions." *TED: Ideas Worth Spreading*, TEDNYC, Oct. 2017, www.ted.com/talks/

scott_galloway_how_amazon_apple_facebook_and_google_manipulate_our_emotions.

Garone, Adam. "Healthier Men, One Moustache at a Time." *TED: Ideas Worth Spreading*, TEDxToronto, Nov. 2011, www.ted.com/talks/adam_garone_healthier_men_one_moustache_at_a_time.

Holmes, Jeremy. *John Bowlby and the Attachment Theory*. Routledge, 1993.

"How Do Men & Women Use Social Media—Digital Branding Institute." *Digital Branding Institute*, 30 Mar. 2016, digitalbrandinginstitute.com/how-do-men-women-use-social-media/.

Ikemoto S (2010). "Brain reward circuitry beyond the mesolimbic dopamine system: a neurobiological theory". Neurosci Biobehav Rev. 35 (2): 129–50.

Lagorio-Chafkin, Christine. "Kevin Systrom and Mike Krieger, Founders of Instagram." *Inc.com*, Inc., 9 Apr. 2012, www.inc.com/30under30/2011/profile-kevin-systrom-mike-krieger-founders-instagram.html.

Macon, Alexandra. "Bumble Founder Whitney Wolfe's Whirlwind Wedding Was a True Celebration of Southern Italy." *Vogue*, Vogue, 5 Oct. 2017, www.vogue.com/article/bumble-founder-whitney-wolfe-michael-herd-positano-wedding.

Martin, Sam. "Claim Your 'Manspace.'" *TED: Ideas Worth Spreading*, TEDGlobal, July 2009, www.ted.com/talks/sam_martin_builds_a_room_of_his_own.

*Meetup*, launched Jan. 2002, https://www.meetup.com/.

McCorvey, J.J. "How Meetup CEO Scott Heiferman Used A Staff Uprising To Create A Better Product." *Fast Company*, Fast Company, 24 Nov. 2016, www.fastcompany.com/3064063/how-meetup-ceo-scott-heiferman-used-a-staff-uprising-to-create-a-better-pro.

McGinn, Brett. "The Problem With Being A Hopeless Romantic." *Thought Catalog*, Thought Catalog, 26 June 2017, thoughtcatalog.com/brett-mcginn/2017/06/the-problem-with-being-a-hopeless-romantic/.

Melville, Katy. "Fine Line Between Pleasure & Pain." *Science a GoGo*, McMurdo Media, 18 Aug. 1999, www.scienceagogo.com/news/19990718214106data_trunc_sys.shtml.

Newman, Meredith. "Report: More Young People Have a Tattoo than Ever before and It Needs to Be Discussed." *Delawareonline*, The News Journal, 22 Sept. 2017, www.delawareonline.com/story/news/health/2017/09/20/report-more-young-people-have-tattoo-than-ever-before-and-needs-talked/682396001/.

O'Brien, Sarah Ashley. "Pickup Soccer's Key Player." *CNNMoney*, Cable News Network, 27 June 2014, money.cnn.com/gallery/smallbusiness/2014/06/27/meetup-startups/2.html.

OkCupid. "10 Charts About Sex—The OkCupid Blog." *The OkCupid Blog*, The OkCupid Blog, 19 Apr. 2011, theblog.okcupid.com/10-charts-about-sex-47e30d9716b0.

OkCupid. "A Woman's Advantage." *The OkCupid Blog*, The OkCupid Blog, 5 Mar. 2015, https://theblog.okcupid.

com/a-womans-advantage-82d5074dde2d

OkCupid. "I Tried To Spice Up My Sex Life With Hygge and Fell Asleep." *The OkCupid Blog*, The OkCupid Blog, 14 Mar. 2017, theblog.okcupid.com/i-tried-to-spice-up-my-sex-life-with-hygge-and-fell-asleep-4ef07a6a67d4.

OkCupid. "Why More People Are Having Sex on the First Date—The OkCupid Blog." *The OkCupid Blog*, The OkCupid Blog, 5 July 2017, theblog.okcupid.com/why-more-people-are-having-sex-on-the-first-date-7330ddbea30f.

"The Pleasure Centres Affected By Drugs." *The Brain From Top To Bottom*, Canadian Institutes of Health Research: Institute of Neurosciences, Mental Health and Addiction, thebrain.mcgill.ca/flash/i/i_03/i_03_cr/i_03_cr_par/i_03_cr_par.html.

*Tinder*, launched 12 Sept. 2012, https://tinder.com/.

Reiner, Andrew. "Teaching Men to Be Emotionally Honest." *The New York Times*, The New York Times, 4 Apr. 2016, www.nytimes.com/2016/04/10/education/edlife/teaching-men-to-be-emotionally-honest.html.

Russo, Miranda, and Tracy Wilcoxen. *How to Get out of the Friend Zone: Turn Your Friendship into a Relationship*. Chronicle Books, 2013.

Seiter, Written by Courtney, and Kevan Lee Read more. "The Secret Psychology of Facebook: Why We Like, Share, Comment and Keep Coming Back." *Social*, 12 Aug. 2017, blog.bufferapp.com/psychology-of-facebook.

Smith, Aaron, and Monica Anderson. "5 Facts about Online Dating." *Pew Research*

*Center*, 29 Feb. 2016, www.pewresearch.org/fact-tank/2016/02/29/5-facts-about-online-dating/.

"Social Media Fact Sheet." *Pew Research Center: Internet, Science & Tech*, www.pewinternet.org/fact-sheet/social-media/.

Stokes, Colin. "How Movies Teach Manhood." *TED: Ideas Worth Spreading*, TedxBeaconStreet, Nov. 2012, www.ted.com/talks/colin_stokes_how_movies_teach_manhood.

Systrom, Kevin. *Instagram*, founded Oct. 2010, www.instagram.com/.

Tech, Omidyar Network | Emerging. "A Conversation with Scott Heiferman, Founder & CEO, of Meetup." *Medium*, Medium, 4 Dec. 2017, medium.com/@EmergingTech/a-conversation-with-scott-heiferman-founder-ceo-of-meetup-f46b6d97d569.

Tepper, Fitz. "Here's Who Fared Best on Dating Apps in 2016." *TechCrunch*, TechCrunch, 3 Jan. 2017, techcrunch.com/2017/01/03/heres-who-fared-best-on-dating-apps-in-2016/.

watchcut. "Kids Tell Their Parents How They Lost Their V-Card | Cut." *YouTube*, YouTube, 19 May 2017, www.youtube.com/watch?v=Xp7eHLH4J-o.

watchcut. "Ilah Tells Her Mom How She Lost Her Virginity | Cut." YouTube, YouTube, 19 Aug 2017, https://www.youtube.com/watch?v=9OsLLOw7WwY.

Webb, Amy. "How I Hacked Online Dating." *TED: Ideas Worth Spreading*, TEDSalonNY2013, Apr. 2013, www.ted.com/talks/amy_webb_how_i_hacked_online_dating.

Wiking, Meik. *The Little Book of Hygge: Danish Secrets to Happy*

*Living*. Thorndike Press, a Part of Gale, Cengage Learning, 2017.

Winfrey, Oprah. "Will and Jada Pinkett Smith." *OWN*.

Zuckerberg, Mark. *Facebook*, founded Feb. 2004, www.facebook.com/.

Made in the USA
Middletown, DE
06 May 2018